# THE Holistic Witch

## CONNECTING WITH YOUR PERSONAL POWER FOR MAGICKAL SELF-CARE

•·•·•

SHAWN ROBBINS
LEANNA GREENAWAY

STERLING ETHOS
New York

An Imprint of Sterling Publishing Co., Inc.



ISBN 978-1-4549-4255-9
ISBN 978-1-4549-4256-6 (e-book)

Distributed in Canada by Sterling Publishing Co., Inc.
c/o Canadian Manda Group, 664 Annette Street
Toronto, Ontario M6S 2C8, Canada
Distributed in the United Kingdom by GMC Distribution Services
Castle Place, 166 High Street, Lewes, East Sussex BN7 1XU, England
Distributed in Australia by NewSouth Books
University of New South Wales, Sydney, NSW 2052, Australia

For information about custom editions, special sales, and premium purchases, please contact specialsales@sterlingpublishing.com.

Printed in China

2 4 6 8 10 9 7 5 3 1

sterlingpublishing.com
Cover design by Amy King
Interior design by Christine Heun

Picture credits – See page 301

# Dedication

To the doctors, nurses, and care workers throughout the world who have stared death in the face during these unprecedented times. Your tireless devotion to the sick, not to mention your bravery and courage, knows no bounds.

We stand among the witches of this world
and send you our heartfelt thanks.
You are an inspiration to us all.

*—Shawn and Leanna*

# Contents

## Part Three: Holistic Home, Garden, and Family



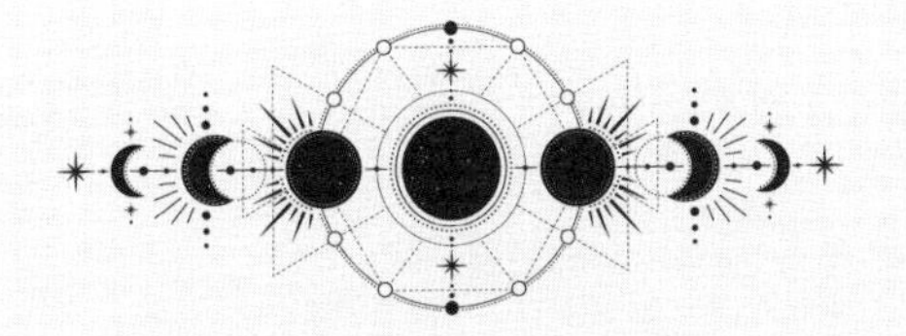

# Introduction

## YOUR MAGICK LIFE FORCE

So many of us take extra-special care with our outward appearance. We pay top dollar for the latest fashions, text our hairdresser for emergency highlights, and hit the gym religiously. And while we talk about how critical it is not just to take care of our physical body, we must also focus on the importance of looking after our soul.

Have you ever thought about what makes someone unique? For a moment, forget about a person's name or how they look. Instead, concentrate on their essence, their life force. It sounds clichéd to say that no two people are alike, or that each person is simply composed of thoughts, actions, and behaviors that are theirs and theirs alone.

But we all share something very important. We have a purpose on the planet and are here for a similar reason. Each of us is on our own personal journey, with our souls evolving at different rates—but at the same time, we have a responsibility to one another. We are all part of the same universe, which in a way makes us part of one another. How we interact with those around us has an impact on how our soul develops, so if we try our best to help—and not hinder—our fellow humans, we can make such a difference in people's lives.

Whether you believe in Wicca or not, within each person a mysterious power resides. Most of the time, as we go about our daily lives, this part of our life force is concealed, but then, occasionally, something unexplained happens that leaves even the most skeptical people scratching their heads. You may have a weird dream that later comes to fruition or you get an extreme feeling that something is wrong. Have you ever met someone for the first time and the hairs on the back of your neck stand on end? You're not sure why, but there is something about this person that rubs you the wrong way. It might be that they're telling you an anecdote, and you immediately know they are not telling the truth. We call these "gut instincts," but really, they are far more than that. These feelings are all-powerful and shouldn't be ignored. Some believe that our guides plant thoughts in our minds to make us aware when something isn't as it should be. Others think that we have the ability to tune into the energies around us, recognizing the positive and the negative vibes. Each one of us possesses this power, but often we shoo it away, thinking we have an overactive imagination.

## HOW TO FIND YOUR MAGICK

Before you can use your unseen attributes to the best of your ability, you must first find out what they are. It's really a matter of going on a quest of self-discovery. Not everyone possesses the same kind of magick and some witches who have practiced for years still struggle with certain crafts. We can look at it from a practical perspective by comparing magickal skills to the specialties of craftspeople who work in the building trade. There are plasterers, carpenters, electricians, pipefitters, and masons—each skilled in their own way, just as each magickal practitioner is skilled in their own particular art. One witch might be a fantastic potion maker, but will struggle with divination, while another might be an excellent tarot reader or have a flair for palmistry but has no success with spellcasting. Everyone's magick is different. It's safe to say that we are all individually good at something, so we must find out what it is we are best at—and only then will we be able to connect to our internal power. The way to unearth your talents is first to try out those practices that you are most interested in. You might have an avid interest in crystals or love to carve your own wands. Your passion could be candlemaking or you might be an expert at creating poppets. Your heart will always tell you which witchy path to follow; you just have to pay attention to the signs and listen to your inner voice.

To find your magick, you have to invite some form of spirituality into your life. It doesn't matter what type of spirituality it is, just as long as you open your heart to a path that brings you in tune with the Universe. For some it might be a religion they feel an affinity with, for others it could be more of an interest in the afterlife. We must take time to sit quietly and think about life in a more spiritual way.

Every person is on a slightly different vibration so each one of us might differ somewhat in our opinions. Dig deep to find your own truth and when something feels right to you, believe it. We were not born onto this earth by accident, so it's vital for us to understand why we are here; why we are living and breathing right now. It's no mistake that you have been given life. You are special and you have been chosen to fulfill some karmic life path, so you must make sure that every minute you live on this earth you are the very best person you can be. This way, you will raise your vibration and ascend to a higher level upon death. We have spoken of this in our other books, but it's worth repeating for those who haven't yet read them. There is a purpose in life. It's not just about going to work, coming home, feeding yourself or the kids, dogs, and cats, and going to sleep . . . it's far more than that. It's about perfecting your soul. You need to get to know your true self, pay great attention to how you are feeling, and learn to trust your gut instincts. When you truly know yourself, you will be able to harness the power within and holistically care for your entire being—and extend those positive vibrations to the world around you.

In order to unleash our inner magick, we must also be at one with ourselves and our thoughts. Meditation is the perfect exercise to enable this. It's essential to do a little bit of meditation every day. You don't need to spend hours and hours sitting in the lotus position, trying desperately to reach a meditative state; simply go to bed half an hour earlier than usual and, as you relax, try to focus.

Another excellent exercise to do when you want to tune into your higher self is to sit very quietly in a room with no distractions. Turn the television or music off and just close your eyes and listen to the silence. After about ten minutes of this, you will start to feel differently. Pay close attention to your thoughts; what are they saying? You might like to do a bit of meditation and imagine yourself somewhere tranquil, like a beautiful lake, an open flower field, or a secluded beach. Picture yourself touching the flora or walking barefoot along the sand. It's at times like this that you can truly connect with your internal voice and unleash its power. (See pages 25–29 for more detailed meditation exercises.)

We need to focus on every single part of our being, from the condition of our bodies to the well-being of our minds. Everyone has ups and downs in life and often, when we are in a negative frame of mind, that can impact our physical health. Whether you're happy or stressed in your current

situation, one thing is for sure: it will change! When life starts to become challenging, negative energy can barge into our hearts and minds, taking control of our emotions and the decisions we make. It can also engulf our souls in a negative fog, which can be harmful to our work life and relationships. Once our mood starts to plummet into a downward spiral, it can feel like it's impossible to break the pattern. The good news is there are lots of ways to prevent that spiral from happening and cast out those negative vibes. First, you must take the reins of your life. This is your existence and your journey, so you have to take control of what happens to you, as best you can. Of course, there will be many things that you cannot influence in life—illness and other people's actions, to name a few—but once you get into the right mind-set, you can banish any negativity around you, replacing it with positive energy.

Most of the time, more than one problem hits us at any one time, leaving us feeling overwhelmed and beleaguered. Trying to eliminate multiple issues at once rarely works so, instead, just address one problem at a time. Be kind to yourself and work within your limitations. The solutions sometimes take time to sort out, so try not to bombard your mind with too much; once you have conquered just one obstacle in your life, you will feel more empowered to work on the next one.

Write down a list of all the things that make you unhappy, such as a difficult relationship with a significant other or a family member, a problematic living situation, or unhealthy eating or sleeping habits. Once you have your list, put them in order of priority. Without focusing on any of the other issues, just focus on the worst of your problems. If your relationship is faltering, try to better communicate your feelings, do something to spice it up, be more loving to your partner, or make an appointment to see a therapist. It's essential to do all of these positive, practical things first, and then give it an extra boost by coupling it with a little magick.

## EACH LIFE EXPERIENCE IS A LESSON

If you have read the other books that we have cowritten over the years, you will know that Leanna has been in touch with her spirituality from a very young age and has spent many years searching for the purpose of her life. After practicing meditation, hypnotherapy, and astral projection, she believes she has found some of the answers. Of course, your truth might be different from hers, which is why everyone must seek their own. Throughout human history, we have come to understand how the physical body functions, but there is still one thing we are trying to fathom: our vital life source—the human soul. The body might become diseased or wear out over time, but the essence of a person is a different matter. Each soul is unique and has its own identity, and everyone's spirit is developing at a different rate. During one of Leanna's hypnotherapy sessions, when she was regressed to a time before birth, she was told that the soul was immortal. Our bodies are just a vessel to carry our souls, and by the time we have finished reincarnating we'll have resided in many forms. We'll all be young, we'll all be old; we'll all be disabled, we'll all be hale; we'll all be poor and undistinguished, we'll all be rich and famous. The purpose of living is to learn and ascend from our experiences. Sometimes we have to undergo some pretty harsh lessons in order for us to grow; this is because we need to thoroughly understand life's tests by experiencing them firsthand.

It doesn't matter if we don't achieve everything that is dealt to us in any one lifetime. Sometimes, it takes many reincarnations to triumph over a set task, but have faith; we will all get there in the end. When you try to balance the physical with the spiritual, it can take time. Use baby steps and be kind to yourself.

Throughout this book, we will give you lots of magickal tips and techniques so that you can begin to embrace your life on a more witchy, spiritual footing. Practitioners across the world will all have their own thoughts and ideas about what witchcraft means to them, and these are ours!

Part 1

# Holistic Energies for Self-Love

# Chapter 1

# The Holistic Magickal Tool Kit

IN THIS BOOK, WE WILL BE DISCUSSING THE OVERALL well-being of a witch and cover many kinds of physical and emotional issues that can be alleviated with a spell or two. Twinning practical techniques with rituals only amplifies the magick and, above all, empowers you, the spellcaster. You don't need to spend lots of money on your tool kit, either: many things can be sourced from Mother Nature. However, you must take time when you are gathering or acquiring your items; each one is very important for your future tasks. Listen to your instincts when you are choosing and if it feels right, then go ahead and use it.

# ESSENTIAL ALTAR ITEMS

Before you perform any type of magick, first you will need to set up an altar—a sacred space that you create as a base for all your spellwork. A small table is okay or, if you are limited for space, you can purchase or make an altar board that can be packed away when you are not using it. Both of us always leave our altars set up in an accessible area within our homes so that we can get to them quickly when need be, but some witches may prefer to keep their practice private.

Over time, you will probably stockpile many items. You might want to buy a special box or small chest to house all your precious things. If not, designate a set of drawers that is specifically used to house all your objects. Following is a list of the key items you will need for your holistic magickal tool kit.

## Altar Cloth

The color of your altar cloth should pertain to the magickal task at hand; for self-care rituals, it's always best to have a yellow or golden cloth covering the surface. This color represents all things that relate to health. White is also an acceptable shade when you are casting any kind of well-being spell. Lavender or deep purple is a good color for spells involving spiritual fulfillment and chakra work.

## Candles

Not every spell calls for a candle, but they are required for many rituals, so make sure you have a stash of different-colored candles in your collection. There are a few varieties of candles you can buy, but the most common is the "spell candle," which measures about 4 inches (10 cm) in length. These work well because there is plenty of room on the wax surface to inscribe your desires. Tealight candles work well, too, as they burn quickly, but they have limited space for engraving. Chub candles, which may be tall or short but are chunky—usually a minimum of 2 inches (5 cm) wide—are excellent for engraving. For spells that don't need inscriptions, you can opt for a small beeswax candle. These are quick burners and useful if you want to cast a last-minute spell.

The most important thing when you're performing a ritual is your intent, so if you condition your mind to believe that your spell is definitely going to work, you give it a far better chance of succeeding. One of the reasons a witch inscribes a candle with her wishes is simply to amplify that intent. So often you might think a spell hasn't worked because you weren't sure of the spelling or the inscription on the candle was so small that you could barely read it. But misspelling or text size makes no difference whatsoever to the outcome. It's all about the intent.

For self-care rituals, make sure you have two large, white chub candles at the back left and right sides of your altar. They will cleanse, bless, and complement any ritual you are performing. The smaller spell candles should be situated toward the front or center of the altar. It's always best to use yellow or gold spell candles unless otherwise specified. Once a spell is complete, the large chub candles can be blown out and relit at a later date.

## Pentagram

The symbol of a pentagram (a five-pointed star) is widely used in ritual magick. If you don't have an ornate one, you can simply draw the image on a piece of paper or print one out from an online source. Always make sure the pentagram is placed on your altar in the upright position, with the top point facing away from you, the two side points left and right, and the lower points at either side on the bottom.

## Quartz Crystal

Quartz is an amplifying stone, meaning that it enhances and projects positive energy to the surrounding area. Having a small piece of clear quartz present on your altar during any spell relating to health and well-being will magnify the magick.

## Ritual Dish

This is a must-have. It's best to use a small dish that is fireproof, as you may need to burn incense or leaves. Don't just grab any old cereal bowl out of the kitchen cupboard; you need one that is sacred and used only for spellcasting.

## Salt

Salt, typically kept in an open bowl, purifies and cleanses your magickal space. Some witches like to have a bowl of sea salt or table salt present on their altar to sanctify their tools. For example, you can rest any crystals you might be using for a ritual on top of the salt to cleanse and bless them.

## Stormwater or Rainwater

Weather witches collect natural rainwater every time there is a downpour, and they transfer it into bottles to use later. During a thunder and lightning storm, the water contains added energy, so make sure to place a sturdy plastic container or bowl outside when a storm is forecast. This water is used for bathing, blessing candles, and in healing lotions and potions.

## Wand

A wand is a necessity for casting a circle at the beginning and the end of your spell. You can purchase some beautiful wands online, or you may fancy having a go at making your own (see chapter 10). If you do decide to make your own, you'll find some great wand-making tutorials on YouTube. You also may want to build a wand collection so that you can choose a wand for a specific spell, depending on the type of wand wood.

## White Feathers

White feathers represent all things spiritual and will help you to call upon your chosen deity before a spell commences. You can purchase these at a store or online, or, even better, use bird-given feathers you find outside.

## OPTIONAL EXTRAS

This is your altar and you are in charge, so any trinkets or charms you have created or found will grace your magickal workspace. Having items present that represent the four elements is a practice widely used by experienced witches and is a nice touch.

- **You could place a small dish of soil or a bowl of pebbles somewhere on the table to signify the earth element.**
- **Athames are wonderful for creating a magickal circle before your ritual begins, and the ones with sharp blades can even be used to inscribe your candles.**
- **A besom or broomstick is often propped up beside the altar, or you might source a miniature broom to rest on the altar's surface. This symbolizes the clearing away of anything negative.**
- **A cauldron works as an excellent container for any herbs you might use. You can even place a florist foam block inside it for holding your incense sticks.**

- **A sacred cup, or chalice, is perfect for holding stormwater and can even serve as a vessel for blessing potions.**
- **Crystals offer so many different properties and you can learn about which ones to use specifically for certain issues in one of our other books, *The Crystal Witch*. Corresponding crystals add extra punch to a spell.**

## WHERE TO PLACE YOUR ITEMS

Traditionally, a witch's altar should face north, but there are really no hard-and-fast rules: your spells will work just as well wherever you orient your altar. Altar placement is personal to every witch, so you must do what you feel. However, you might want to put your representative objects on the following points of your altar to help your spell along:

### North–Earth

**CANDLE COLORS** Any shade of green

**ITEMS** Pentagrams • salt • dirt from outdoors • metals or ceramics • herbs and flowers • seeds • dried foods • stones or pebbles • crystals

### South–Fire

**CANDLE COLORS** Red, orange, and brown

**ITEMS** Candles • lighters • matches • volcanic stones • spices • orange or yellow flowers • images or figurines of cats, lions, tigers, or dragons

### East–Air

**CANDLE COLORS** Yellows, cream, and gold

**ITEMS** Feathers • athames • swords, knives • wands • wind chimes • bells • incense • anointing oils • images or figurines of angels, fairies, or deities and of birds, dragonflies, or butterflies

## West–Water

**CANDLE COLORS** Blue, turquoise • white

**ITEMS** Chalices • stormwater or rainwater • seashells • crystal ball • mirrors • seaweed • sand • wine (white, red, or rosé) • images or figurines of mermaids, fish, dolphins, or whales

Whenever you cast a spell, take a photo of your altar so you can refer to it again in the future. These pictures can be placed in your journal.

## THE BOOK OF SHADOWS JOURNAL

Most witches like to record their magickal practices so they can list the ingredients they used or, later, compare the outcomes of spells. The journal or notebook used for this purpose is called a book of shadows or grimoire. You really don't have to spend a lot of money—any hardcover journal or notebook will do (a sturdier hardcover is best because it will get thumbed a lot over time). I (Leanna) have oodles of these books, each one different but all packed full of information. In one book I might have a list of all the moon phases for that particular year, so I know the best time to cast a spell, and in another, I'll make a list of herbs that I like using, writing the magickal correspondence next to each one. I also like to start a new book at the beginning of every year. I might write down my dreams or any psychic experiences I might have, as well as recording any spells I have done, with a small section at the bottom to log the outcome of the ritual.

Most witches love to collect all kinds of books on Wicca and end up having an extensive collection in their bookcase, but when you want to perform a particular spell and you need to quickly check what ingredients are best to use, it can be difficult to remember just what information is in which book—especially if you are like me and have hundreds of them. To make this easier, while I am reading I copy down anything I might find interesting or useful into one of my own books of shadows. It's straightforward to reference, and above all, you're able to easily access the knowledge of other witches and combine one spell with another—this often adds more impact. You can purchase some adorable journals or notebooks today, and loved ones are never stuck with what to buy you for birthdays or yuletide—they can always source a pretty jotter.

## How Can It Help Me to Grow and Learn?

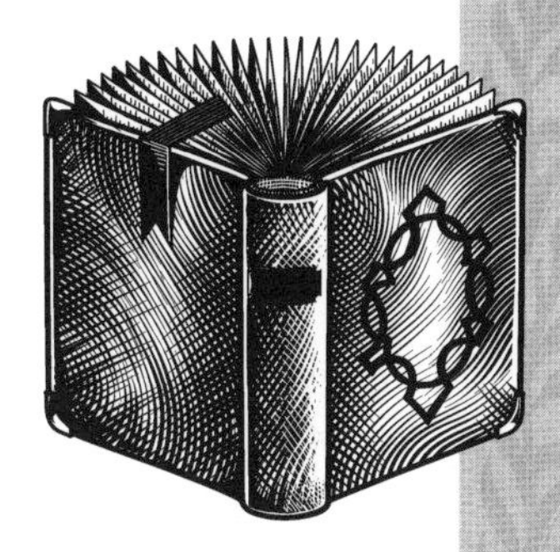

Sometimes, I might just opt for an early night in and spend an evening with all my journals on my bed. If you record your spells and make notes about each one, it can really help to jog your memory. Oil blends and mixed herbs can be easily forgotten, so you'll have this wonderful reminder at hand any time you need to reflect.

## Can I Share It with Others?

I've never been one to keep my spell formulas a secret. Nowadays, witches love to share information with others, many joining online forums or creating blogs and YouTube channels, giving demonstrations that might help other witches. It's a fantastic way to share good ideas, and there is always something new to learn.

When you come to create your altar, remember that there is no right or wrong way. Yes, it's wonderful to practice tradition and set everything out and have your items perfectly positioned, but sometimes you might just want to cast a quick spell without spending hours and hours in preparation. There have been many times when we have simply just lit a candle in the living room or the kitchen to help along a situation and the spell has worked just fine. It really all boils down to your intent and your mental mind-set, and often we do not need a barrage of objects to help us do that. Just go with the flow and do what feels right!

## Chapter 2

# Spiritual Self-Care: The Magick Within

MAGICK IS AS MAGICK DOES. THAT IS, YOUR SOUL AND spirit have everything to do with what you seek and what you produce. Someone who has a chip on their shoulder might seek revenge or otherwise wish harm on others. On the other hand, someone who has a light spirit and not a care in the world is more likely to turn their attention and intention toward bettering the world around them. This isn't meant to judge, but to explain the differences in magickal pursuits. (Yes, there really are good witches and dark witches.)

The truth is that we all have our times when nothing is going the way we want and hope flies out the window. It's part of being human. In those moments, we have a choice: we can collude with the negative energy, or we can reach for something better. Both options are available to us, no matter what's happening in our lives, and both take the same amount of effort on our part. It's a matter of focus.

Many of us have been faced with uncertainty recently. Instead of giving in to anxiety, this is the perfect time to bring fearful thoughts into the light, to face them, and send them packing. In this chapter, we'll talk about ways to heal your soul and maintain a constructive spirit even in times of distress.

## PRACTICING GRATITUDE

You've seen the memes and posts on social media that say, "There is always something to be grateful for." Well, that's not just a passing sentiment—that is the absolute truth! There are times when it's hard to express gratitude or to even think about what you might be grateful for, but, again, we're talking about effort; if you're scared, angry, or anxious, you'll have to dig a little deeper.

We asked people in our communities what they are thankful for. Here are some of the answers:

- **Good friends**
- **Family**
- **Waking up this morning**
- **Reliable transportation**
- **Food in the house**
- **Helpful people in the community**

- **Having a job**
- **Being able to get out of bed**
- **Pets**
- **Being able to create**
- **Favorite songs**
- **Sunrises/sunsets**
- **Spring rain**
- **A warm, dry home**
- **Being in nature**
- **The ability to see**
- **Books**
- **Modern medicine/good health**

This list could go on for pages and pages, but you get the idea. Even the seemingly smallest things, like getting out of bed in the morning or being able to fix yourself a nice breakfast are events to be acknowledged. One respondent said, "I was having a terrible day, and then I saw a man getting out of his car and into a wheelchair all by himself, and I thought, 'I don't even think about how easy it is for me to get around. I've been in a bad mood all day, and here's this person who could feel like his life is so hard—and yet he's smiling and waving to people in the parking lot.' That brief experience gave me a new perspective. I think about that every single day—not that I pitied this man, but that his spirit was stronger than any physical limitation."

We all tend to take certain things for granted, which is exactly why it's important to stop and think about all that we have and are able to enjoy. Take some time to think about your life, your accomplishments, your goals, your abilities, and the things you've overcome. Make your own gratitude list and celebrate it! Personalize your ceremony by including the very things you're most grateful for. For example:

- **If you are overwhelmed** by the love you feel for your family and/or friends, invite them to a prayer or ceremony circle. Start by expressing your feelings for them and encourage each person to do the same.

- **Give thanks for nature** by taking a walk or a hike without any distractions. Give yourself the opportunity to take in the sights, sounds, and smells of the forest, desert, or beach—wherever your wandering spirit leads you!

- **Before you roll out of bed** in the morning, take a minute to offer thanks for your health, your job, your home, or your dog waiting for you beside your bed.

- **Meditation** is always a wonderful way to connect with your spirit guides, angels, Universe, Spirit—whatever you call your higher power—and express gratitude. After you give thanks for specific people, places, or things, you may want to add an additional request: "Please open my eyes to the things I haven't given thanks for. Let me know their value in my life." (See pages 4 and 25–29 for more about meditation.)

## Mystical Elements for Gratitude Rituals

You can always incorporate mystical elements into your thanksgiving ritual, like the following:

- **White candles** are used to promote peace and harmony and represent the unity of spirits.

- **Other candles** represent (quite literally) light shining through the darkness.

- **An angelite crystal or pendant** boosts the spirit and gives strength to your intention.
- **Amethyst** chases away anxiety, fear, and sadness. Negative energies don't stand a chance when amethyst is on the scene!
- **Rose quartz** is the stone of universal love and acceptance. This is a perfect stone to use if you've had a major life change and you're searching for the positive aspects of your new situation. It also promotes spiritual healing and inner peace.
- **Add some aromatherapy.** Lavender promotes relaxation. Frankincense improves concentration. Citrus oils lighten the mood.

We'll talk about facing particularly challenging situations—those that seem to have no silver lining—in the next section. For right now, take some time to explore the types of rituals that might work best for you. Write down the elements you'll need—people, stones, music, candles—and then make your ritual a reality.

## RESTORING HARMONY

Some of you might be saying to yourselves, "It's easy for you to write about gratitude, but my life is never easy! Nothing goes the way I want it to. I have nothing to be thankful for." Indeed, there are situations that can bring us to our knees, spiritually speaking, and this is even true for folks who seem to have more than their fair share of blessings. It's in these moments that it's especially important to find a shred of brightness or hope to cling to, to carry us through until the crisis eases.

When we get knocked off our spiritual center, we can either wait for a rebalancing to happen on its own or we can take action. Your choice in the matter can lead to drastically different outcomes for years to come. There's no doubt that looking for a bright spot in a terrible situation is challenging, to say the least. It takes real effort to fight the urge to collude with negative energy. On the other hand, it takes very little effort to find a dark spiritual space. That darkness, however, can irrevocably harm your soul if you allow yourself to linger there too long.

In addition, our physical health is related to our spiritual health. Long-term anxiety, fear, or anger take a toll on the body and can lead to insomnia, high blood pressure, digestive issues, trouble with concentration and memory, headaches, backaches . . . a plethora of aches, pains, and illness.

We understand the importance of maintaining energetic health. Let's talk about how to restore well-being to a stressed or damaged spirit.

## Meditation

Taking just several minutes a day to hit a spiritual pause button can help give you a new perspective, especially if you're feeling particularly emotional, angry, or stressed. For many witches, meditation is like taking a step outside of the situation where they can escape to their spiritual place, so when they're ready to come back to spellcasting, they are doing so with a refreshed mind.

You should try to meditate for at least ten minutes every day. Meditation has a multitude of health benefits for the body and the mind:

- Lowers blood pressure and improves cardiovascular health
- Reduces anxiety
- Improves decision-making
- Provides an overall sense of well-being
- Spurs creativity
- Improves sleep

Meditation requires no equipment other than your time, effort, and intention. Simply set aside ten minutes when you can focus on your objective—whether it's pure relaxation, positive thoughts, improved creativity, or empowering one of your altar tools by holding it as you meditate. You can lie flat or sit on the floor on a carpet or mat (if there's a risk of falling asleep, sitting may be best), practice deep breathing, and begin (some suggested techniques are found on page 4 and in spells throughout). Some elements to try in your meditative practice include:

- Connecting with your spirit guides
- Offering gratitude
- Visualizing positive outcomes
- Exploring your dreams and desires
- Repeating a mantra

In addition to the direct benefits associated with meditation, many people find that improvements in mood, sleep, and health lead to improvements in relationships, work output, and a better outlook on life in general. There's just one problem: Some people find it extremely difficult to quiet their mind and enter into a meditative state. They find that they are too distracted by other thoughts and throw the whole idea of meditation out the window, so to speak. These people might benefit from guided meditation. In this practice, you listen to a narrative that leads you through a landscape or situation. For example, the narrator might begin by saying, "Imagine yourself as a leaf floating on the breeze. Feel how light you are as you twist in the wind . . ." From there, the tale continues. Your job is to focus on the narrator's words to visualize and feel what the story suggests.

You can find lots of examples online just by searching guided meditation. You can also be the narrator for someone else, simply by engaging your creative side. This might work wonders for a child who has trouble settling down at bedtime or for a loved one who isn't feeling well.

## 8–2–8 Technique

For a quick meditation, try the following:

Prepare a quiet, comfortable space for yourself, free from distractions. Sit in a chair. Close your eyes and engage your senses. Feel the seat under you; listen to your breath; smell the air. Slow your breathing. Inhale for a count of 8; hold for a count of 2; exhale for a count of 8. Repeat.

As you feel yourself starting to relax, visualize yourself physically releasing negative emotions, like a vapor coming off your body. Alternatively, imagine breathing in refreshing new energy and breathing out harmful energy. Concentrate on inviting healing energy into your aura.

Repeat this practice daily. End your meditation by offering gratitude for just one or two things at first. With each day, try adding something new to be thankful for.

## 4–7–8 Technique

The 4–7–8 technique is another great exercise to try. Gradually breathe in through the nose on the count of 4, then hold your breath for the count of 7. Slowly, breathe out through the mouth on the count of 8. Repeat this cycle, concentrating the entire time on your breathing. Notice that when you inhale your breath is cooler, and as you exhale it gets warmer. Your mind might start to meander, and you might start thinking of everyday issues or problems. If this happens, envision those intruding thoughts being placed in a container of sorts. You can address all those problems and concerns at another time.

After a while, you may start to feel floaty; this is a prelude to astral projection and is nothing to worry about. What do you feel? Can you hear voices in your head? What might they be telling you? Some people report that they hear ethereal music or bells ringing in the distance. Concentrate on the sounds and listen. Often, visions will appear behind closed eyes, which you might later want to record in your journal. Some people have even described seeing snippets of their past lives during this type of meditation.

Keep a journal of your rebalancing meditations, adding a short note about how you're feeling that day, what methods work best to help you relax, what you envision during your meditation, and the like. In time, you will see a pattern emerge: healthier emotions before meditating (because you're reaping the benefits from the prior day's practice) and greater insight following the session.

## Mindfulness

We hear the word *mindful* a lot these days. We're told to act mindfully, eat mindfully, communicate mindfully. What does this mean, though?

Truth be told, there are different ways to be mindful, but all of them focus on engaging in the present moment and paying attention to what we're doing. Everyone is so busy multitasking and always thinkingabout what needs to be done next that many of us move through every single day on autopilot. When a witch is faced with this situation, meditation is a must so that they can redirect their focus and concentrate on what's important.

Think about some of these situations:

Have you ever asked someone their name and forgotten it almost immediately?

Do you ever drive to work, the store, or a friend's house and realize that you have no recollection of the route you took?

How many times a day do you walk into a room and say to yourself, "What was I coming in here for?"

Have you ever had someone recount a conversation they had with you and think to yourself, "This sounds exactly like something I might have said, but I don't remember saying it to this person"?

These are all pretty minor events, but they're a good indicator that you need to slow down and pay more attention to your life!

Buddha apocryphally said, "Do not dwell in the past. Do not dream of the future. Concentrate the mind on the present moment." Taking that idea to the extreme, we need to acknowledge that even five minutes ago is the past. Five minutes from now is the future. We need to focus on the here and now, which is not easy in this age of technology and always wanting and needing more, more, more.

One way to take yourself out of a moment of distress caused by worry or anxiety (or, in the extreme, a panic attack) is to engage as many senses as possible. For example:

- **Feel the chair you're seated on.** Is it soft or hard? Warm or cold? Comfortable or uncomfortable?
- **Smell the air.** Is there a candle burning in your home? Are there springtime scents in the air? Can you smell your dog's wet hair?
- **Can you taste anything?** Did you have a cup of coffee recently or something with garlic for lunch?

- **Focus your vision on one thing,** like a clock or a pleasant sight, a flower, or a picture of a loved one.
- **What do you hear?** Really try to listen for background sounds, like a clock ticking or a truck on the highway.

Studies have shown that engaging the senses in this way distracts the brain from worried thoughts. As a result, blood pressure drops, your breathing slows, and you begin to feel calmer. This has a cascade effect, because once you feel calm you will likely continue on that path until you're fully relaxed. But the opposite it also true—when panicky feelings start to take hold, that triggers even more panic. That's why it's best if you can catch those feelings early on and shut them down.

You might also want to try a mindfulness walk, which is similar to the exercise we just talked about, except you're mobile. Choose a walking area where you're comfortable (for example, a city person probably wouldn't feel safe all alone on a country road, and vice versa), and, as you walk, take note:

- **What do you feel?** Is the air warm or cold? Humid or dry? Windy or still?
- **What do you smell?** Is someone having a bonfire out in the country? Or, in the city, can you smell the bakery's fresh bread or the café's coffee aroma?
- **What do you taste?** Again, this might be a remnant of a meal you had earlier, or, in the case of strong scents in the air, you might actually taste a smell!

- **What do you see?** In this exercise, you're going to do something a little different and not focus on just one thing, as in the mindfulness practice above. What is catching your eye on this walk? Are you looking around you, or have you been looking at the ground?
- **What do you hear?** There are so many sounds outside that you will most likely have a plethora of noises to listen to. Again, try to focus on the sounds that we don't always pay attention to—traffic, the breeze, birds chirping, or voices coming from a storefront.

## Forest Bathing

Shinrin-yoku, or forest bathing, is a Japanese mindfulness practice that evolved in the 1980s to restore harmony to the soul. Part of the theory behind forest bathing is that because humans evolved in nature, this is where we need to go to recharge and rebalance. The sights and sounds of the forest are therapeutically essential when we feel low and out of sorts. Nature heals the mind and regenerates the spirit.

Forest bathing has been shown to lower blood pressure and also decrease depression, anxiety, and insomnia. It provides us with the opportunity to clear the mind of psychic cobwebs and lay the foundation for peaceful thoughts and practices.

Forest bathing is a dynamic experience—no two visits will feel exactly the same. Although the forest that you visit may be hundreds of years old, the life within it is constantly changing. Animals come and go, depending on the time of day or the season. In temperate zones, the trees put on a show with vibrantly changing leaves in spring, summer, and fall, before the forest enters the bareness of winter. Sun, rain, snow, and wind change

the feel and smell of the forest. Even though you might have a favorite spot, it may look different every time you visit.

You don't have to be in a thousand-acre wood to reap the benefits of forest bathing. You can do it in a park or in your backyard—anywhere you can surround yourself with nature for a period of time. Here are some tips to make the most of your experience:

- **Leave your phone behind.** This is your time to reconnect with the natural world and there's nothing less natural than the phones we're all so dependent on! The goal is to be mindful and present. You don't need to post this experience on social media, nor will you need to take pictures. Just be in nature.

- **Move freely, without expectation.** Wander through the park, woods, or your yard with one simple intention: enjoying the moment. Relax. This is your time.

- **Fill your senses.** Take the time to observe the world surrounding you. Feel the breeze, smell the earth, listen to the animals scurrying around. Hold a cool stone, rub your hand along the rough bark of a maple tree. Absorb the peace of these moments, feeling it wrap around your heart and your mind. Birdsong is believed to influence the way leaves grow—think about the effect this beautiful sound can have on your soul.

- **Pause. Have a seat.** Don't rush through this experience on your way to an appointment or an errand. Find a comfortable spot and relax for a while. You might want to bring a blanket or a chair if you're headed to the park.

- **Be as silent as possible.** If you take a friend with you on this adventure, try to keep your chitchat to a minimum until after you've left the forest or park. This will allow each of you to fully experience nature on your own terms. Compare notes afterward: Was there anything that stood out to either of you? Did either of you notice something that the other person completely missed?

You can bring some of this practice into your own home by creating a nature altar. Include bits and pieces of things you find along the way (without disturbing or destroying the natural environment, of course):

pine cones, fallen leaves, stones. You can also incorporate a houseplant, a succulent, or a bonsai tree to re-create the greenery of being outdoors.

## REFLEXOLOGY: THE PRESSURE IS ON!

We've been talking about the body, mind, and spirit working together as a unit. When one of them is "off," the others will fall out of balance as well. Think of the body as a network of energetic lines running every which way, but not in chaos—in perfect order. Along these networks are certain pressure points that conduct energy to specific points. These spots on the hands and feet are easily accessible and make up the practice of reflexology. Many witches are now learning this art; Leanna knows a few who have studied it and have incorporated it into their craft.

Reflexology has been shown to be a safe and effective means for reducing stress and increasing endorphins, the feel-good hormones. When endorphins increase, in turn, pain is decreased, sleep is improved, and your mood starts to perk up as well. Suddenly, your perspective on life is different, and you're able to find solutions to problems that seemed insurmountable just a few days ago!

**ANXIETY RELEASE FOR ANXIETY,** try massaging what is called the Heart 7 (HT7) point. To find it, hold one hand with the palm facing up. On the pinky side of the hand, go to the crease where your palm ends and your wrist begins. You'll feel a little indentation there. That's the HT7 point. Massage this for a minute, and then switch over to the other wrist.

**STRESS AND TENSION RELIEF** The reflexology point for your brain is in your big toe! To alleviate stress, rub your big toe with your thumb, up and down, but also move your thumb from one side of your toe to the other. Repeat for 30 seconds to a minute, and then repeat on the other big toe.

If you find that you hold a lot of tension in your shoulders, neck, jaw, or head (resulting in tension headaches), try the temporal area reflexology point, which is along the inside edge of your big toe. Press your thumb on the toe, right along the nail, and move it down until you reach the base of the toe. Now pick your thumb up and repeat this motion for 30 seconds to a minute and repeat on the other big toe.

**CLEAR WORRY** The spleen is associated with worry, overthinking, and brooding thoughts. Clearing the spleen of "stuck" energy will help to move these thoughts along as well. This point is found on the sole of the left foot only. To find the exact spot, imagine dividing your foot into quadrants, with a line down the middle and a line horizontally. The spleen spot is along the outer edge of the left foot just above the imaginary horizontal line. Press your thumb into this spot and rub up and down for 30 seconds to one minute.

**PEACEFUL REST** If you find that sleep is elusive, try the Kidney-1 point, which draws excess energy from your head and mind and allows you a peaceful rest. To find this spot, imagine again dividing the soles of both feet into quadrants. The Kidney-1 point is found in the top inside quadrant (toward the inside of the foot, not quite halfway down the sole of your foot, toward the middle). Press your thumb in this spot and move it in a circular motion, continuing to move it down about a half inch for about 30 seconds to one minute.

Try making a ritual of your reflexology practice by pairing it with relaxing music, a soothing bath, a candle, or aromatherapy (see pages 37–39 for more on scent).

## Flood Your Senses with Scent

Aromatherapy dates back to the ancient Egyptians, Babylonians, Indians, Chinese, and Greeks, who offered aromatic flowers, oils, and incenses to their deities and used them in perfumes and in medicinal treatments. In the Middle Ages, the perfumed scent of dried herbs and flowers was believed to ward off "miasma" in the air that caused plague and other illnesses. People carried or wore herb mixtures, or burned them as incense. The celebrated Persian physician and thinker Avicenna began distilling essential oils in the eleventh century. Centuries later, French chemist René-Maurice Gattefossé wrote about the subject in 1937 in his treatise Aromathérapie: Les Huiles Essentielles, Hormones Végétales (*Aromatherapy: Essential Oils, Plant Hormones*).

In recent years, aromatherapy has reemerged as a legitimate means of enhancing and healing energy. In fact, you've likely seen an essential oil diffuser somewhere in your daily travels—at the doctor's office, in a little boutique, at the spa, in a friend's home. Many mental health professionals offer aromatherapy as an adjunct treatment. For example, when you arrive for an appointment, your therapist might ask if you'd like some calming lavender, either in a diffuser or on a cotton ball. Massage therapists also regularly work healing essential oils into their massage oils and lotions.

An aromatherapist works with a person's specific lifestyle, astrological signs, personality, and preexisting conditions to develop a custom blend of essential oils for that person to mend the body and the spirit. Some aromatherapists swear by using astrological signs as a starting point for finding the most effective essential oils for a person. What do the stars say about your best scents?

**ARIES → ROSEMARY** Aries is a go-getter and doesn't have time for nonsense. Rosemary has a sharp, direct scent that provides a boost to Aries's already jam-packed day. Mix with some lavender or bergamot to help tame tension.

**TAURUS → ROSE** Taurus comes charging into any situation with confidence and boldness—just like the strong scent of roses. Both are uniquely strong and cannot be overpowered. Use sandalwood and frankincense as companion oils if feelings of doubt and insecurity start to creep in.

**GEMINI → BASIL** Strong and versatile, basil mirrors Gemini's intensity and habit of being involved in everything. This scent can be used to boost a weary mind but is equally at home in the kitchen in a variety of recipes. Try using clary sage and rose to bring some focus to your busy days.

**CANCER → BLUE CHAMOMILE** This sign is all about nurturing others, and blue chamomile matches that energy perfectly. It has a calming nature, like Cancer, and is perfect to soothe the stomach issues that this sign is prone to. Add some cinnamon oil to shake things up and provide a boost of energy.

**LEO → JASMINE** There is nothing shy about Leo, which is what makes jasmine the perfect scent for this sign. It's indulgent and bold, just like the Leo personality. It's also a definite seasonal scent, reflecting Leo's endless-summer mind-set. Bergamot and ylang-ylang are good companion oils, as they help to ease Leo's occasionally intense irritation.

**VIRGO → LAVENDER** Virgo personalities are lovely and loving, like lavender itself. They are the first to respond to a crisis of any sort, and the last to consider themselves a hero. This sign is associated with the mother goddesses of the harvest season. Peppermint and cedarwood are nice companion oils to give Virgo a boost of concentration and healing energy to their overgiving selves.

**LIBRA → GERANIUM** Libra personalities are usually focused on what's fair, what's right, and how to balance the scales. Geranium is used as a balancing scent in aromatherapy, which makes it perfect for this sign. If you find that geranium is too strong for you, add some palamrosa—this is a type of grass that may be more to your liking.

**SCORPIO → PATCHOULI** Scorpios are known for their deep, sensual energy. Patchouli has been used as an aphrodisiac for centuries, making it the perfect scent for this sign. Ginger and lemon are excellent companions, as they add a zing of freshness and light to patchouli's earthiness.

**SAGITTARIUS → BLACK PEPPER** Sagittarius doesn't beat around the bush, and neither does black pepper, with its stimulating scent! Sagittarius is full of energy and sometimes says things before thinking. Rosewood can help to smooth out those overexcited edges and bring Sagittarian energy back into balance.

**CAPRICORN → VETIVER** This sign is like an oldest child: responsible, overachieving, and well rooted. Vetiver is an earthy scent that plays on the ambition and serenity of Capricorns. Amyris mixes well and encourages relaxation when Capricorn has been working too hard!

**AQUARIUS → NEROLI** Aquarians often appear to be distant, off in their own little worlds—lost in deep thought and happy with their own company. Neroli is a great oil for meditation, to help Aquarius sort out all those thoughts. Marjoram is a good addition and helps to soothe the anxiety that many overthinkers are prone to.

**PISCES → LEMON BALM** Pisceans are the ultimate water sign, and lemon balm has a high water content, making them a perfect pair. This sign is highly compassionate and absorbs a lot of dark energy from others, and lemon balm helps to ease anxiety and depression. Cinnamon pairs well with lemon balm and encourages Pisces's natural psychic abilities.

## QUANTUM MECHANICS: THE NEW MAGICK

We've talked a lot about meditation, spells, and bringing thoughts into reality in this chapter, and this discussion wouldn't be complete without touching on quantum mechanics, a theory concerning atomic and subatomic particles in physics. The word *physics* might transport you back to science class, but we promise you won't be graded on this! In fact, once you understand the concept of quantum mechanics, you'll be amazed at how you can control the energy surrounding you.

Quantum physics states that, when viewed at the subatomic level, particles don't behave the way we would otherwise expect them to. There is a famous experiment called the double slit that demonstrates this:

- A laser beam is shined through a plate with two narrow parallel slits, and the light flows through the plate onto a screen.
- Most people would expect to see two lines of light on the screen, but this isn't what happens. The light appears in shorter stripes.
- This is because the particles of light waves interfere with each other and cancel each other out at certain points in their respective waves.

Light is energy, and we are all made of energy and surrounded by energy, which can also be manipulated by certain forces, including our consciousness and our intention.

This is pretty heady stuff, but what it means for us is that we can manipulate forces by focusing on what we want to bring about. This is the definition of magick, after all, and when we talk about meditation or the

use of crystals, chants, or music in spellcasting, this is what we're doing: affecting the forces and energies that are already surrounding us.

Try these fun and easy experiments:

- During meditation, send love to someone who has been unlovable lately.
- Focus on something you want to materialize. Believe it has already happened.
- Create a policy of all-positive thoughts for 24 hours. If you hear negative news, try to find a silver lining. See what happens.

Remember that we are all part of one unified energy, and we all have a part in the form it takes. Let's each do our best to make it as beautiful, prosperous, and light as possible.

# The Most Important Person Is You

Everything we've discussed in this chapter relates to taking the best care of your physical and spiritual self.

This isn't an indulgence or something that any of us should feel guilty about. We can't take care of anyone else if we ourselves are not well. We can't effect great changes in the world if we're coming from a place of hurt and fear. It's essential for us to look within and heal those old wounds before we can move forward effectively and with an understanding of our motives.

Maybe you realize that you don't take care of yourself, that you are stressed, that you're pulled in ten different directions every day. "How can I change this?" you ask. "My life is so busy. I don't have time for meditation!" The answer is simple, and maybe a little infuriating: make time. Meditation can take just five or ten minutes. Take a walk in nature on your lunch break or sit outside after you've put the kids to bed. Add aromatherapy to your bath or dab a few drops on a cotton ball and keep it on your desk. Build a self-care altar in your home and include pictures of you at your happiest and most energetic. Realign your chakras and cleanse your aura (see chapter 3).

There's a wise old saying: You can't pour from an empty cup. Heal yourself, and watch your world follow suit.

Chapter 3

# Chakras, Auras, and Smudging

**THE WORD CHAKRA MEANS "WHEEL" OR "TURNING" IN** ancient Sanskrit. Yogic Hindu and Tantric Buddhist traditions describe chakras as energetic centers or energy wheels, "spinning" like gears at specific points in the human body. There are seven main chakras, from the top of your head to the base of your spine, and each one is associated with a specific area of the physical body as well as with a spiritual attribute. When a chakra becomes blocked or unbalanced, your physical health as well as your spiritual health may be affected.

If each gear is turning as it should, the body is in balance and you're feeling pretty good. But let's say that a gear is stuck or it's missing one of its "teeth" or is otherwise damaged—the body will become out of sync and, as a result, you will feel out of sorts. The energy that is ordinarily flowing around your body effortlessly will slow down or even block up completely. It's absolutely vital that while we look after our physical self, we also pay attention to our internal energy fields.

The seven chakras are as follows:

### ROOT CHAKRA

At the base of the spine. This energy center keeps you feeling grounded and safe. If it becomes imbalanced, you will be filled with panic or entering survival mode.

### SACRAL CHAKRA

Located in the lower abdomen, below the navel. This is a pleasure center and is related to healthy relationships and creativity. An imbalance here leaves you feeling uninterested in your usual activities, often resulting in a low sex drive. It can also have the opposite effect, where your emotions are out of control.

### SOLAR PLEXUS CHAKRA

Situated in the upper belly, right below the diaphragm. This is the energy center that feeds your confidence, power, and wisdom. When this chakra is out of whack, as with the Sacral Chakra, it can also make you feel as though your emotions are haywire. Normally, calm people find themselves flying off the handle or experiencing bouts of irritability.

## HEART CHAKRA

As you would expect, this chakra is centered in the chest, and feeds love, compassion, and healing. If this point becomes misaligned, you could experience sadness or jealousy, or feel unloved and overly critical of yourself and others.

## THROAT CHAKRA

Situated in the neck, this is the chakra that feeds your voice, opinions, and communications. Imbalances here will make you feel as though you can't express yourself well or that no one is acknowledging your opinion. You might feel judged by others, which makes it more difficult for you to speak your truth.

## THIRD-EYE CHAKRA

Found in the center of the forehead, slightly above the eyebrows. This feeds your awareness and insight. Blockages here may manifest as feelings of fogginess or you might be overly inclined to daydream. You could also have difficulty making decisions or wrapping your head around logic.

## CROWN CHAKRA

Positioned at the top of the head. This is the center for spirituality, full consciousness, and enlightenment. When this chakra is off track, you will feel distressed and disconnected from everyone and everything, as though you can't set or follow goals.

When all these centers of energy are whirring along happily, positive energy will be moving through your body and spirit at an optimum pace. You'll feel great! You have goals, hope for the future, healthy friendships, and your emotions are in check.

If you have any of the following feelings, it is likely that one or more of your chakras is out of sync, and will be either spinning slowly or it has some spiritual negativity or "gunk" attached to it. When this happens, it may throw the rest of your chakras off-balance, because they work together as a single unit.

- You're feeling anxious.
- You're having trouble relaxing.
- You feel as though you don't trust anyone.
- You can't focus.
- You're having arguments with everyone.

## CHANGING YOUR ENERGY WITH CHAKRA HEALING

The chakras work together, so when one is off-kilter, the rest of the system starts to lag. And while all the chakras can benefit from some TLC at any time, it's vital to address the root of a spiritual slowdown to prevent a chakric roller-coaster ride.

Each chakra vibrates at its own level and is associated with different colors and methods for healing.

**ROOT CHAKRA** Associated with the earth, for grounding. Walking barefoot in the yard or park, lying on the ground, or spending time outdoors will help to bring this chakra back into balance. This point is associated with the color red, so dress in red clothing and eat red fruits and veggies to help bring it back up to full speed. You can also place a red crystal, like a ruby, in the area of your root chakra during a meditative session.

**SACRAL CHAKRA** Associated with water, for flow. Take a swim, a bath, or even soak your feet to start healing this chakra. The sacral point responds to the color orange, so carrots, orange peppers, oranges, tangerines, or mangoes will help with healing, as will orange stones or crystals like carnelian or amber.

**SOLAR PLEXUS CHAKRA** Associated with fire. Sit in the sun or build a bonfire to bring this chakra into balance. Foods like bananas, turmeric, pineapple, or corn are beneficial for healing, as are crystals or stones like citrine or yellow jasper.

**HEART CHAKRA** Associated with air. Try to get as much fresh air as possible, and practice deep breathing during the day: Inhale, slowly, for a count of eight. Hold it for three seconds, then release the breath completely, again counting to eight. This chakra likes the color green, so incorporate green foods like lettuce, avocado, and broccoli in your diet, and use a green stone like jade or emerald during meditation.

**THROAT CHAKRA** Associated with spirit and the ether. Spend time outside soaking in the sun and fresh air to get this chakra back into balance. This chakra responds to blue foods like blueberries, blue corn, or blue cheese. Use blue stones or crystals like sapphire, blue topaz, or lapis lazuli for meditation.

**THIRD-EYE CHAKRA** Associated with light. Open up the blinds, light candles, or get out in the sunshine to reawaken this chakra. This chakra is associated with the color indigo, so you can try foods like blackberries, concord grapes, or purple kale. Stones like iolite or sodalite will work well during meditation.

**CROWN CHAKRA** This center encompasses all the others, so addressing the whole of your being is essential for opening this chakra. In other words, you must care for your mind and body with the full range of nutrients, exercise, and rest! To heal this chakra, the color violet will help, so lepidolite and amethyst are good choices for meditation. The Crown Chakra is also associated with white, so quartz and diamond are also beneficial.

## Soothing Chakra Ritual

Here is a simple ritual to soothe your chakras and harmoniously realign them. You will need to gather crystals or stones in the colors associated with each chakra:

**MATERIALS**

Red stones for Root Chakra (ruby, red jasper, or garnet)

Orange stones for Sacral Chakra (sunstone, carnelian, amber)

Yellow stones for Solar Plexus Chakra (citrine, yellow jasper, tiger's eye)

Green stones for Heart Chakra (jade, emerald, adventurine)

Blue stones for Throat Chakra (sapphire, blue topaz, or lapis lazuli)

Indigo stones for Third-Eye Chakra (iolite, sodalite)

Violet or white stones for Crown Chakra (lepidolite, amethyst or quartz, diamond)

**RITUAL**

Create a comfortable spot to lie down. Place the crystals in the general vicinity of each chakra. Close your eyes and visualize each energetic wheel spinning, paying close attention to the chakra that's off-balance. Visualize this chakra receiving healing energy from the others, until you see it coming out of its hibernation—spinning slowly at first, and then humming along at normal speed with the others.

Place your hand on this chakra to seal in the healing energy. Say a prayer of protection and thanks. Continue this ritual for several days until the balance is fully restored.

You might also want to visit a shaman if your chakras need some tender loving care from an expert. Shamans are trained in identifying and healing damaged energetic fields, and they may want to cleanse an ailing chakra with a particular crystal. Reputable shamans can be found through your local New Age shop.

## Reiki for Chakra Balancing

Reiki is a gentle means of healing the physical body as well as the spirit, which makes it ideal for moving around chakric energy. This practice was developed by a Japanese Buddhist in the 1920s and can be used either to heal oneself or to heal someone else.

Hand positioning is the driving force behind Reiki healing, and for the purpose of chakra healing, there are several useful placements, listed below and opposite, along with the associated chakras. You can either place your hands directly on your body or just above. Either way, remain mindful of the energy you are healing. Visualize the chakras spinning as they should and restoring your spiritual side to good health.

**HANDS ON EYES** Third-Eye Chakra

**HANDS ON HEAD/TOP OF CROWN** Third-Eye or Crown Chakra

**HANDS ON FOREHEAD AND BACK OF HEAD** Third-Eye Chakra

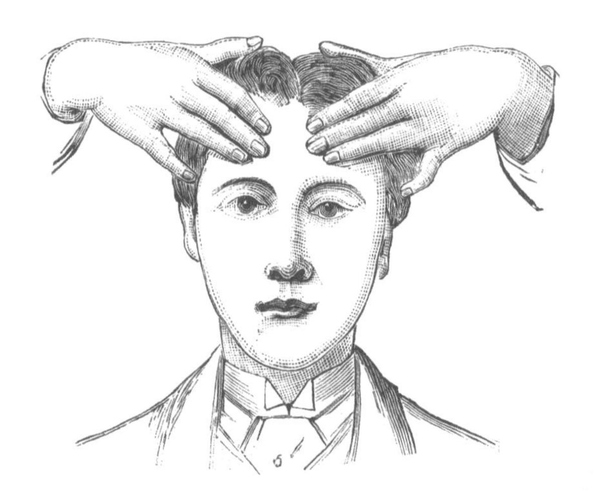

**HANDS ON THROAT AND BACK OF NECK** Throat Chakra

**HANDS ON HEART** Heart Chakra

**HANDS ON STERNUM/UPPER ABDOMEN** Solar Plexus Chakra

**HANDS ON LOWER ABDOMEN** Sacral and/or Root Chakra

Memorize the following mantra to say either aloud or to yourself while you are working with chakras:

> *To change the way this body feels, first I must attempt to heal,*
> *With help and blessings from the divine, my chakras will align.*

If you are using Reiki to heal general energy, you might first do a "body scan," which will indicate which areas need healing. If you follow the guidelines above, you may already have an idea of what type of energy is stuck and where, which makes it a little easier to jump in and focus on the specific point. Whether you lay your hands directly on the area, or just above your body, they should remain in place for four to five minutes. You may feel a warmth, a vibration, or a "shift," indicating that energy is becoming unblocked and balance is being restored.

When you attempt to heal chakras, keep in mind that it took some time to slow down the system, and it will take time and effort to get all the energy centers operating at their optimal levels again. Keep at it and know that each passing day will bring more healing.

Think of this as a deep cleansing for the spirit—sort of like a fancy spa treatment, except instead of a pampering energizer for your skin, your soul will emerge feeling fresh!

## CHANGE YOUR BODY'S ENERGY

Our life force is called different things in different cultures. In Chinese medicine and philosophy, it's called qi or chi. In India, it's prana. Kundalini is a close equivalent from Hindu teachings. Other terms include *ki* (Japanese), *orenda* (Iroquois), *mana* (Polynesian), and *ase* (Yoruba).

Each of these teachings have subtle differences, but they fall under the larger umbrella of unseen "subtle energy," which is what keeps our mind, spirit, and body flowing as one cohesive unit. If humans are composed of energy, and energy can't be created or destroyed, therefore it merely changes form. There will be times when our energy levels are high and times when our energy takes a nosedive. We must learn to harness our positive energy to get the most out of it, while also managing dark and negative vibrations that may be swirling near or even inside of us.

Witches see the life force as a ball of pure energy. Your energy is at the mercy of your moods, so it's very important to keep a lid on any overflowing emotions. If a person is continually in a bad mood or they are a grumpy sort who is prickly and difficult to be around, their energy will remain mostly negative. For those who have a sweeter disposition, other people will enjoy being in their company as they hold the power to transform their own energy with their positivity. Energy is contagious. We throw it out there every moment of the day.

Many witches are sensitive to other people's life force and often guard against people who possess a dark energy by carrying or wearing a protective crystal, such as black obsidian or black tourmaline. This doesn't mean that all those souls who possess a dark energy are bad people. Often, if a person behaves in negative way, they are covering up a certain pain or insecurity in their lives by acting badly. Never retaliate in a negative way; instead, try to show compassion and empathy and stay calm. Throwing out negativity will only merge their negative energy with yours and create a far worse scenario. We all hold the power to change our own energy and to also have an influence on others. It's very hard to be hateful toward someone who is being nice to you. Try to be patient with others and understand why they might be behaving in that particular way. At the same time, it is vital for us to work on ourselves to purify the energy we possess.

The practice of working with your body's energetic field is called "energy medicine." Utilizing specific techniques, you can learn to recognize, work with, and change energies that are not serving you well. You can also learn to identify and release energy that is "stuck" and dragging you down.

Energy medicine is an entire field of study; shamans and other practitioners spend years learning about the unseen systems of the body, and you might be interested in learning more or visiting a professional for a more thorough session. In the following pages, you'll get an overview of how energy flows, what you might experience if the flow is blocked, how to release negative energy, and how to achieve energetic balance—all by working with your aura.

## See and Soothe Your Aura

Have you ever walked into a gathering and just instantly clicked with someone you barely knew? Or have you been introduced to someone who gave you bad vibes before they had a chance to say a word? Well, those good and bad vibes are real! While chakras are the energy centers inside the body, each of us also has an aura, which is the energy surrounding our physical being. When the aural energies between two people are in sync, you feel an affinity for someone; when your aura is at odds with another person's, you might get an unpleasant feeling that leaves you feeling wary of the person and ready to walk in the opposite direction.

The word aura is from the ancient Greek and Latin words for "air." Everyone has an aura with both the shape and color of the aura indicating a person's overall health and state of mind. In a healthy person, the aura is an egg-shaped halo; in a person who is experiencing emotional or physical distress, it may lose its shape. In every person, regardless of health, the aura has several layers:

**ETHERIC LAYER** Extends about 2 inches (5 cm) from the physical being. Associated with physical health.

**EMOTIONAL LAYER** Extends 2–4 inches (5–10 cm) from the body. Connected to feelings.

**MENTAL LAYER** Extends 4–8 inches (10–20 cm) from the physical body. Relates to thoughts and intelligence.

**ASTRAL LAYER** Extends 8–12 inches (20–30 cm) from the body. Represents a connection between heaven and earth.

**CELESTIAL LAYER** Extends 24 inches (60 cm) from the body. Indicative of the person's ability to connect with the spiritual world.

Each layer of the aura is composed of colors, and, like the chakras, auric energy can be diminished or get stuck in one or more of the various layers. However, auras are prone to more frequent and rapid changes than chakras. For example, a bad mood or a minor illness can change the dominant colors of your aura, but your aura is likely to rebound in a day or two.

The colors visible in auras are listed below with both positive and negative attributes:

**DARK RED** Energy, devotion, willpower

**RED** Sexuality, competitiveness, aggression

**CLOUDY RED** Anger, resentment, holding grudges, obsessive thoughts

**PINK** Love, psychic energy, sensuality

**ORANGE** Curiosity, good health, vibrant spirit

**ORANGE/YELLOW** Logic, orderliness, perfectionism

**YELLOW** Positive energy, light spirit, creativity

**LEMON YELLOW** Cynicism, egotism, critical view of others

**LIGHT GREEN** Innocence, healing

**GREEN** Harmony, intelligence, indicates a natural healer

**DARK GREEN** Jealousy, resentment, greed, suspicion

**TURQUOISE** Serenity, peace, healing nature

**BLUE** Loyal, sensitive nature; integrity; communicative spirit

**INDIGO** Artistic, quiet spirit; clear-minded

**VIOLET** Charming, alluring nature

**GRAY** Lack of trust and/or blocked energy fields

**BROWN** Fear of sharing truth or confidences with others

**BLACK** Deep resentment and negative feelings, unforgiving nature

**SILVER** Wealth and luck, abundance in every form

**GOLD** Spiritual protection

The brightness of the colors indicates the level of energy. The brighter the color, the stronger the vibration. A bright aura can indicate an energy that has been active for a long time, or a new energy that is particularly intense. Most of us will show only a few colors at a time, but highly evolved people may have the entire rainbow humming in their auras!

Most aura experts believe that we are all born with the ability to see auras, but we lose that gift by the time we are school-aged. Leanna has always been able to see them, and first discovered her ability when she saw the headmaster's aura while he was onstage during a morning assembly. It was probably visible because he was standing in front of a solid-red, velvet curtain; when there is a distinct block of color behind someone, or if they are wearing clothing with no patterns, the aura will stand out. If you have lost the gift, it is easily awakened by practicing the techniques below:

- Have a friend stand in front of a white or very light-colored wall or a sheet draped over a door.
- Make the light comfortable for your eyes and be prepared to adjust it if you aren't seeing the aura.
- Have your friend stand still against the white background.
- Relax. Practice deep breathing. Let your eyes unfocus as you look at the outline of your friend.
- After a short time, you should begin to see their aura. Not every color may be represented, but you will be able to pick out two or three shades.
- To view your own aura, follow these same steps but use a full-length mirror. Alternatively, place your hand on top of a white sheet of paper and follow the steps to relax your eyes and see your colors!

Auras can also be visualized with aura photography. A psychic or intuitive photographer places sensors on the subject's skin, and then processes the energetic readings from those sensors through a specialized camera. The psychic then interprets the colors and provides an intuitive reading for the subject.

Although your aura may change from day to day, many readers believe that the aura is also like the rings of a tree, and periods of trauma and growth are readily visible as well. Many aura readers believe that physical and mental illness starts with a weakness in the aura, so take note of what you are seeing. Negative energy or dim colors could indicate the need for self-care and reflection on what the possible causes might be.

## Cleanse the Negative

What happens if you don't like what you see in your energy field? First of all, don't panic. Remember that your aura is susceptible to frequent changes, more so than the chakras. But if, for example, you see brown, black, or gray in your aura, there is a simple ritual to follow for cleansing.

**MATERIALS**

Epsom salts or baking soda

6 drops lavender essential oil

A white candle

### RITUAL

While filling a bathtub for a soak, toss in a handful of Epsom salts or baking soda (or both). When the tub is full, add 6 drops of lavender oil. Before stepping into the tub, light the white candle, which is representative of purity.

Close your eyes and practice deep breathing as you view your aura changing in your mind. Picture yourself surrounded by a rainbow and let yourself feel that positivity.

Step into the tub, continuing to envision your aura changing in a positive manner. Soak for 20 minutes. Let the negative energy be drawn away by the Epsom salts or baking soda.

Rinse yourself with the showerhead or clean water from the spigot when you are finished soaking.

## Crystal Aura Cleanse

You can also cleanse your aura using crystal energy. Clear quartz crystal is a powerhouse stone, as it has neutral properties and can be used for just about any purpose, including cleansing.

### MATERIALS

2 pieces of clear quartz

### RITUAL

Hold a crystal in each hand and visualize your aura changing from dark to light. Incorporate the colors you want to see in your vision.

Slowly, move one hand up and down the side of your body, then wave it up and down the front of your body. Do the same thing with the other hand on the opposite side of your body.

Give yourself 24 hours before viewing your aura again. Repeat the cleansing ritual as needed.

## Smudge Your Spirit Clean

Another way to purify your mind and soul is to perform a smudging ritual with sage. You can find premade smudging bundles (or smudge sticks—we'll use the terms interchangeably) at a New Age shop or you can order them online. As this ritual involves smoldering herbs, it is best to perform it outside if possible (if you live in a area that is not prone to brush fires). If done indoors, go to an area in your home without carpets and away from flammable materials. In both instances keep a bucket of water or a hose close at hand.

### MATERIALS

A fireplace or grill lighter

A sage smudge bundle/stick

A sweetgrass bundle

A fireproof bowl

## RITUAL

Prepare your mind by setting an intention. Visualize the aura you want. Is it bright yellow? Orange? Pink? Rainbow-colored?

Practice deep breathing as you ask Spirit or the Universe to bring you into the energy you seek. Feel your energy shift as you see the change happening in your mind.

Light the sage smudge bundle/stick with the lighter and blow on it so it produces smoke.

Wave the stick around your head, enveloping yourself in the smoke. Continue to wave it so that your body is surrounded by the smoke. Set the bundle aside in the fireproof bowl, and visualize negative energy being pulled away from you. Picture it dissipating with the smoke. Then extinguish the stick by pressing the smoldering tip against the bowl until the smoke no longer rises.

Light the sweetgrass and do the same thing—surround your body with the smoke, set the stick in the bowl, and visualize all positivity and light energy coming to you. Then carefully extinguish the stick as noted above.

You can smudge yourself as often as you want or need. Remember to always open and close your ritual with a prayer of gratitude and a statement of intention.

Chapter 4

# The Witching Hour: Dream Symbols and Sleep-Well Spells

EVER WONDER WHY THINGS GO BUMP IN THE MIDDLE OF the night? It's common for witches to wake at 3 a.m. on the dot, and the hour between 3 a.m. and 4 a.m. is often called the "witching hour." Odd occurrences can happen any time from midnight to 3 a.m., although some people consider 3 a.m. to 4 a.m. to be the most magickal. A regular person might be stirred awake by a weird or vivid dream during the night and just shake it off as nonsense or not pay any attention to it; however, with witches, it's a little more complicated. Many witches are extra perceptive and psychic, and, for them, a strange dream can leave them feeling odd or confused when they awaken. Some are compelled to seek out a dream interpretation book to understand what hidden message the dream might be trying to convey. Because witches typically meditate and use the nighttime to connect with their guides and the astral planes, oftentimes they will have more profound dreams than others. This is because regular meditation and spiritual communication raises an individual's consciousness, leaving them open to mysterious and unexplained incidents that often occur at night.

## DREAM WEAVERS

It is a widespread Wiccan belief that our spirit helpers visit us when we are sleeping. They can also alter our mind-set during sleep so that when we wake up we might feel differently about something or we

may suddenly become inspired to try something new. Guides and spirit helpers find it much easier to talk to us when we are in the sleep state because our vibration is so much higher and we are less distracted and preoccupied with mundane day-to-day things. Often, they will send us messages by way of a dream; sometimes the messages within the dream are straightforward, while other times they are more complex and need some kind of interpretation. Your guides might also use this time to give you physical healing. This can sometimes be felt as a vibration in your mattress or cold, pleasant, shivery spasms occurring throughout your body. If you are feeling unwell, ask your guide to heal you when you are sleeping—you might be surprised how much better you feel upon awakening.

But what about some of those dreams that you can't fathom? You will find below and through page 74 some interesting interpretations of the more common dreams we tend to have and how they can be messages from the spirit world, giving us knowledge of how to approach certain problems, alerting us to changes we need to make, or sending us needed love and support.

## Abandonment

This is a common dream in which a person might feel isolated and might be searching for a partner or a family member. They might be wandering around from room to room in a house or roaming the streets of a large city, seeking a certain someone. This dream means that you are fearful of rejection and are nervous about being abandoned. Perhaps your relationship is on the rocks, or you are worried that you might lose your job. Your guide is trying to help you decipher your emotions so that they can send you healing and comfort.

## Baby

When a baby appears in a dream, it is a good omen and promises new beginnings for the dreamer, especially if the baby is laughing or smiling. It can also predict the birth of a child within the family and the blessings and uplift that a new baby brings. If a witch dreams of a little one who has already passed over, the child could be coming into her dream sleep to say hello. This tells the mother that she will see her child again in the spirit realm when it's her time to pass. Another theory is that babies represent birth and new beginnings so you might be entering a new phase in life where all obstacles that have previously hindered you will be lifted. The message this dream brings is to be bold and take a step forward.

## Caduceus

In Greek mythology, the caduceus—a rod entwined with two snakes under a pair of wings—is a staff carried by the messenger god, Hermes. It is a symbol of commerce, although it is often used as a symbol of medicine (instead of the more traditional staff of Asclepius, a wingless, single snake–entwined staff named after the Greek god of medicine, Asclepius). To see this symbol in dreams can be a warning of some ill health to come and to take better care of your body. It is a message that you should drink more water and less alcohol, eat a more balanced diet, get more sleep, or exercise more often. If someone else is in the dream, the health problem could be linked to them. The caduceus may also represent a healing guide for the dreamer.

## Death

To dream of your own death can be quite scary and is obviously very worrisome, but much like the death card in tarot, it can indicate the end of one phase and the beginning of another, heralding positivity and transformation. If you dream about a deceased relative or friend, they could be making a connection to send love and optimism your way. Because our vibration is higher when we are sleeping, our loved ones in spirit find it much easier to communicate with us during sleep. When you awaken, try to remember the dream and write it down in your book of shadows. Often, loved ones will bring a message.

## Eagle

All birds are "messengers" and are considered good omens. To see one in a dream may represent a freer time to come with no restrictions. Also, the higher self will be awakened to learn new and positive things to elevate the soul. Perhaps some kind of superior magick will be given to help you soar. If the eagle is chained, then there will be a need to get rid of people or restrictions in your life that are holding you back.

## Falling

This is one of the most common dreams, and most people will experience a dream of falling at some time in their lives. If you are frightened or ill at ease, or feeling that your life is out of control, this can be the reason for the falling sensation. Another explanation is that when our spirit leaves the body to embark on an astral projection, rather than the soul floating upward out of the body, it actually falls down through our back and then rises upward from the side. Many times, this experience happens just as we are falling asleep, and we wake up with a jolt.

### Falling and Soaring

When you dream of plummeting at a fast rate and then suddenly soaring upward with elation and freedom, this is also thought to be related to astral projection. Once you have mastered this, you have successfully left your body, and it is possible to go anywhere you please. (See pages 75–77 for more on astral projection and traveling, and dreams of flying.)

## Gift

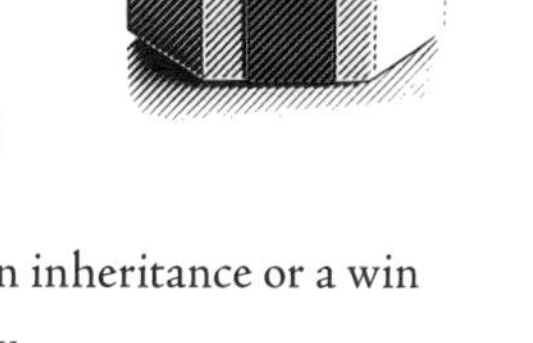

To receive a gift in your dreams is a very positive omen and foretells that your karma is good and that progress is being made. The Universe is happy with how you are conducting your life and they are sending you blessings. It can also indicate a new time of happiness, where unexpected money could appear—an inheritance or a win might be around the corner to ease financial instability.

If you are giving someone else a gift, you must enlighten a person with knowledge or maybe help them if they are starting out in a new home. Give them a useful present or pass on something that you no longer need.

## Hair Loss

To dream of your hair falling out means that you may be worried about something. You may be concerned about world events or are fearful for someone you love. You may have a problem in your life that you feel you have no control over. In these times, ask your guide before you sleep to grant you the power to change things.

## Hauntings by Lesser Entities or Ghosts

It is common for psychic witches to see ghosts or the ugly faces of demons and devils of all kinds in their dreams. These entities can seem to appear right in front of your face and are quite scary, feeding off your fear. They intrude into your dreams from the lower astral planes and are inquisitive about your magickal energy. Psychic children sadly have the same problem, so teaching your child to be unafraid is imperative.

For little ones who have night frights (and for you as well), a Himalayan rock salt crystal lamp can be a real help in their bedrooms at night as it emits calming and peaceful energies. Best to buy one with a dimmer switch to regulate the light for them. Lavender-smelling bed linen is a great help, too, and so is summoning the Archangel Michael for their protection each night.

## Jacob's Ladder

To dream of a long ladder is a good omen for the dreamer—especially if you are ascending it. One step at a time shows progress, but at a steady pace. To step up two or three of the rungs in one go represents quick advancement in your career or in your spiritual development. If you should slip and fall down the rungs, you might fall from grace or embarrass yourself in some way.

## Love

To dream of being in love with another person who you are not romantically involved with at present or whom you have no romantic feelings for while awake indicates that you have some kind of karmic history with them. You have been connected to them in another life. The message in this dream is that every person you spend time within during your life—however long or short the time is—is part of your spiritual development in one way or another.

## Mansion

To dream of a mansion or a large house is a positive dream and could signify a move. The more rooms in the building, the greater the experiences that lie up ahead. Changes are afoot, and you will finally be moving forward in a positive manner. A house can often represent the soul, so if you feel cramped in your dream, you might need to spread your wings and make some new friends to inspire and uplift you.

## Nakedness

Do you have secrets? Is there something you simply can't talk about? Oftentimes, dreams of being naked can mean that you are feeling exposed or are worried about being unprotected. Perhaps hidden truths will finally come out, and problems will be shared. You might also be worried about making a fool of yourself in company or be nervous about an upcoming presentation in front of a large group. The dream is telling you to have confidence in your abilities and not to be bothered by what others are saying about you.

## Ocean

If you dream of walking on a golden beach with a calm blue sea lapping over your bare feet, that is fantastic! It's a splendid omen and means that you are at one with the Universe. If you decide to swim right out into the ocean in the dream, in real life you need to be a little more daring and try new things. If the waves are high, dark, and threatening, you must be careful not to stray too far from those you love. If you feel you are going to drown, in reality, you have too much going on and you are in over your head.

## Pets That Have Passed

Cherished pets and familiars will often appear in a dream by way of touching base with you. During astral projection, it is not uncommon for your old friend to join you on your adventure. Often, they appear in dreams to give comfort, especially if you are still grieving for them. It is also not unusual for your pets to appear a little differently than how you remember them. They may appear larger, more colorful and vibrant, or even have braids and flowers entwined in their fur.

## Power Animal

If you dream of a wonderful large creature, your power or spirit animal could be paying you a visit. From the moment they are born, witches have a spirit animal. Your spirit animal will stay with you throughout your life to protect you. It will be able to converse with you on many levels and steer you in the right direction when you need guidance. One of its tasks is to protect you in dream sleep from sinister lower astral creatures and unpleasant spiritual entities who might even try to enter or "walk in" to your body when you astrally project (see page 75). Try to remember every little detail of a power animal dream, as there is always a message.

## Queen

To see a queen in your dreams sends a powerful message, especially if you are conversing with her. It shows that you have the ability to mix with anyone and to be proud of the way you have progressed through life. Your soul is now becoming refined and great wisdom is in place, so feel free to speak your truth; others will listen and grow from your knowledge.

## Rainbow

To dream of a rainbow is fortuitous, and means that your money situation should start to improve. You will soon be able to treat your family and friends and let them share in your good luck, and a huge burden will be lifted from your shoulders.

## Saint

To see a saint or a holy person in your dream is an indication that you are being visited from another world. If you are depressed, feeling lost, or in mourning, a divine being has come to reassure you that all will be well in the end, and that you should not give up hope.

## Songs and Music

As you become more psychic as a witch, your guides, gods, and goddesses will connect with you in dream sleep with songs and music. If you hear a song that you know in a dream, as soon as you awaken, write down the lyrics; when you read them back later, they might contain a message or hold some other significance. as quite a lot of information can be gleaned from the verses. It is best to record the words in your book of shadows for future reference. Getting messages like this is very special.

## Soul Mate

To dream of a soul mate is a suggestion that your twin flame is reaching out to you from the spiritual planes. You will know if you are in their presence because you will feel an overwhelming love that will leave you not wanting the dream to end. This situation is quite rare, because often we are not allowed to reincarnate with our twin soul. We become too wrapped up in them and avoid other people whom we otherwise might need to spend more time with on our spiritual quest.

Dreaming of your soul mate may set off a yearning that can take weeks to go away, and might leave you looking at your present partner differently.

## Teeth

This dream holds several meanings. In British folklore, it can be an omen that someone is going to die or news of death might be imminent. In other cultures, it may indicate that the dreamer is feeling insecure. If you dream that your own teeth are rotting, then there is a need to pay attention to any bad habits that might be destructive to your health. Spitting out teeth in a dream could be a warning not to gossip, as it will come back to bite you with a vengeance, causing arguments and upsets.

## Visitor

If a visitor comes into your dreams, you must first decide whether or not the person has a good vibe about them. Does the person seem friendly or is there a sinister vibration coming from them? Witches have a magickal aura that attracts spirits wandering the ethereal planes like moths to a flame (see page 75).

### Positive Visitor

Positive visitors are spirits simply passing by just to say hello or to tell you that they are fine and happy in a different dimension. It could be a member of your family or someone you once knew. Or a positive visitor might be one of your guides who has appeared to soothe you and tell you not to worry. (*Note:* Guides often appear in your dreams in everyday clothes—you will know they are one of your guides as you will instantly like them and feel comfortable with them.)

### Negative Visitor

Always listen to your subconscious. If you have even one doubt that the person in your dream should not be trusted, then you are psychically tapping into their otherworldly energy and are being given a sign.

Always be polite and step out of the negative visitor's way. If you have no control in the dream and the person decides to hang around you anyway, the next night before going to sleep, tell the entity that they are not welcome and not to come back. You can also do the Pre-Sleep Protection spell on page 77.

## Wail or Lament

To hear a sad wailing could be an omen that someone in your life, either a friend or family member, will have to go through a harrowing time and you might be called upon to help. If the face of the person is shown to be wailing, then it will be applicable to them. It may also be news of death if the wail is followed by crying.

## X-ray

If you dream of being x-rayed, it could be a strong indication to take care of your health. Perhaps do a detoxification the following day, or make a point of drinking more water or eating a healthier diet. It would be a good idea to establish a better nutritional plan for your family and pets.

We have just touched upon a few dream interpretations here, but there are hundreds of books and sources of information available if you want to explore this further. We like to think that the witching hour is the most magickal time of day; a time when we step out of our physical selves and are free to explore our subconscious, spiritual side. Pay attention in the twilight hours and when you awaken in the night, this semi-sleep state is the perfect time to connect with your guide. Say hello to them and ask them to protect you.

## ASTRAL PROJECTION

The soul can leave the body when we sleep and fly around to all manner of places. If you have ever dreamt of flying, this is a sure sign that you are more than likely astral traveling. These kinds of dreams can be exhilarating and fantastic; imagine holding your arms outstretched and skimming across the ocean or weaving in and out of buildings or trees. As lovely as out-of-body experiences are, you do have to safeguard yourself before venturing off to some faraway place. Without protection, it's possible that when your soul leaves your body you might encounter a disruptive or lesser-evolved soul that can perform something called a "walk-in." This is where the spirit of another entity can enter your body while you are on a spiritual vacation. Don't be too alarmed, as it's quite a rare occurrence. But, unfortunately, there are some nasty spirits out there who are drawn to psychic people—almost as if we emit a light that they are drawn to like moths.

For years, Leanna has suffered from sleep paralysis, an unpleasant, frightening experience where the entire body is paralyzed and you feel as if someone were sitting on your chest. Sometimes, you can actually see monster-like creatures while you are in this state, and it takes a great deal of determination to wake yourself up. Doctors ascribe sleep paralysis

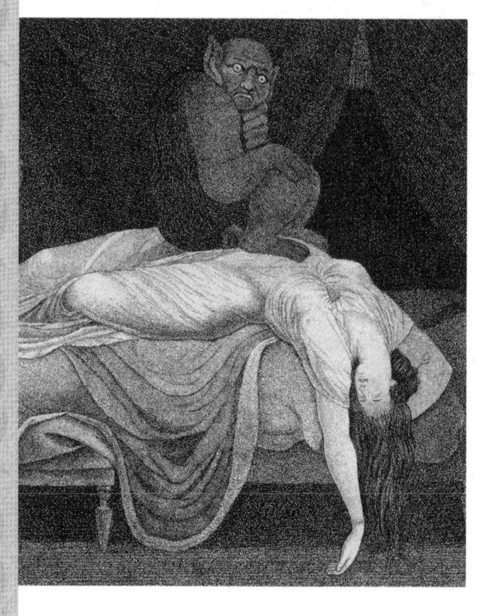

and associated nightmarish hallucinations with waking up while you are still in REM atonia (the natural muscle paralysis that always occurs during the rapid eye movement sleep stage). Yet we feel that the psychic experience aspect of the phenomenon should not be ruled out. Strangely, when Leanna mindfully summons the Archangel Michael for protection during one of these awful experiences, or she tells the frightening spirit in no uncertain terms to depart (usually with a profanity or two), it immediately goes away. Whenever you encounter one of these creatures, show no fear. They love it if they get a rise out of you. Remember, they can't hurt you; they just want to scare you. If you confidently tell them to get off, they will disappear in an instant!

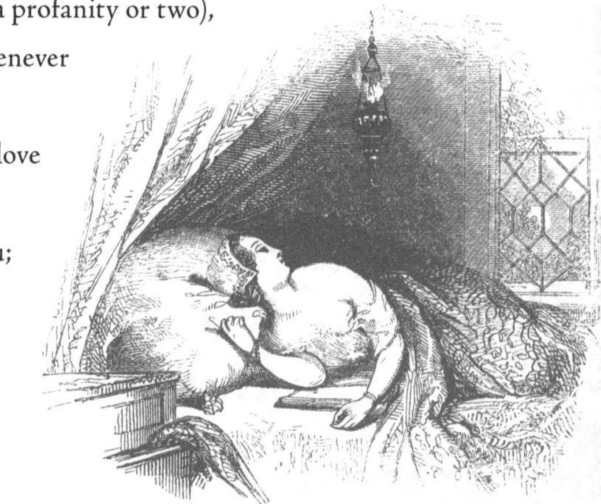

## Pre-Sleep Protection

To safeguard yourself, every night before sleep or after meditation, perform a short protection ritual. That way if you do go jet-setting off to the astral plane, there will be a spiritual sentry somewhere guarding your sleeping form.

### RITUAL

Lie on your back with your hands resting lightly on your stomach, and completely relax. You will know when you are properly relaxed because your mouth will fall slightly open. Concentrate on your breathing for about a minute, and in your mind say this mantra over and over before you drift off to sleep:

*"My guide, my keeper, stand by me,*
*Let my dreams be perfect and trouble-free.*
*Shield my body, protect my soul,*
*Allow me to be in full control."*

Usually, after repeating the mantra three or four times, you will have fallen into a peaceful sleep. Also, this mantra is especially helpful if you wake up in the night and can't fall back to sleep.

## Sleep-Well Spell

There are times in life when you want to bring the energy down a notch, particularly if you need a good night's sleep. Whether you are a chronic insomniac or you tend to lose sleep only when you're stressed, you know how frustrating it can be to have an exhausted body and a mind that can't shut itself down! Here is a ritual that will help.

## MATERIALS

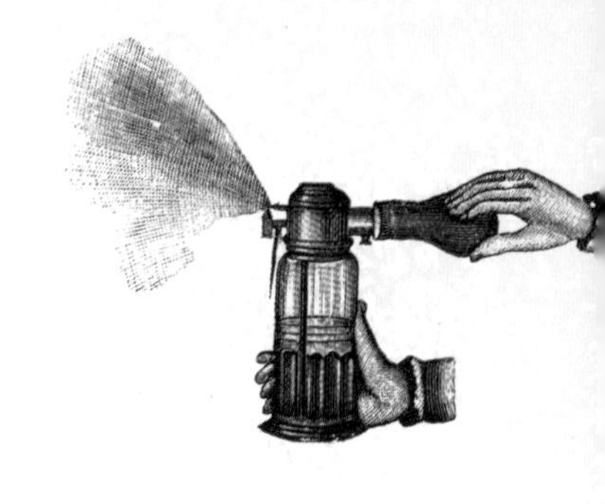

- 14–18 drops lavender essential oil*
- 2 tablespoons vodka or witch hazel
- 3 ounces water
- A small spray bottle
- Vanilla-scented candle
- Epsom salts

## RITUAL

During the daytime, mix 8–10 drops of the lavender oil with the vodka or witch hazel and water in a small spray bottle.

To start yourself on the path to a restful night, spray your bed linens with the lavender spray.

Light a vanilla-scented candle and place it in your bathroom. Fill your bathtub and sprinkle in a handful of Epsom salts and 6–8 drops of lavender essential oil. As you sprinkle the salts and oil into the tub, inhale deeply and say:

*"Restful slumber come to me,*
*Let my mind sleep peacefully."*

Repeat this as you soak for 15–20 minutes, practicing deep breathing.

During this time, stressful thoughts or beliefs that you will not be able to sleep may enter your mind. Let them linger for a moment, but then visualize yourself placing them into a beautiful container and putting a lid on it tightly. The container holds ideas and thoughts that you can deal with tomorrow. Imagine handing this container off to your higher power or mentally stow it away in a closet until the morning.

When you are finished in the tub, rinse off with clean water to wash away any lingering negative or overactive energy that might keep you awake. Blow out the candle.

As you climb into your bed, continue your pattern of deep breathing and your restful sleep chant. Imagine all of the things you are grateful for. Let tomorrow's worries come to you during daylight hours when they are less likely to seem overwhelming.

****NOTE***: Other essential oils you can substitute for lavender oil include the following: cedarwood, chamomile, frankincense, valerian, vetiver, and ylang-ylang. Write down what you've used in your book of shadows so that you can repeat a winning recipe!

## Thank-You and Good-Night Ritual

Another ritual that will help to quiet your thoughts all the way to dreamland involves expressing gratitude. This is a nice way to focus your mind on the positive and on the things that are going well in your life, as opposed to allowing yourself to slide into worry as soon as your head hits the pillow. You can use this ritual alone or in conjunction with a bath, pillow sprays, or other spells.

### MATERIALS

A pen

3 small slips of paper

A jar or box

### RITUAL

After you've prepared yourself for bed, write down the three best things that happened to you that day or something positive that has happened to someone you care about (for example, you might have given a great presentation at work or your child may have had an exceptionally good day at school). Using the example of your child having a good day, perhaps they have been having trouble with peers or a teacher and this issue has been weighing heavily on your mind. Jot down your feelings about the events you are writing about and take time to express your gratitude to the Universe, God, your angels, Spirit, or whomever you give thanks to.

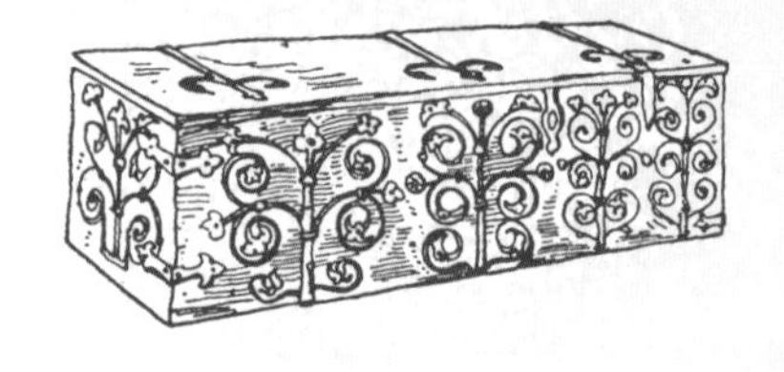

Write your words of gratitude on the slips of paper. As you finish each one, hold it between the palms of both hands pressed together, and say:

*"For what you have brought to me this day,*
*I am truly grateful."*

Place each slip of paper into the container after you offer up your thanks.

When you are finished, place your hands on the container filled with your words of gratitude. Take a moment to consider the magnitude of all that has been given to you.

Take ten deep breaths, saying, "Thank-you" aloud with each exhalation.

When you close your eyes in bed, envision your heart being open to the wonderful possibilities headed your way the following day. If you are a chronic worrier, anxious thoughts may find their way into your imagination. That's all right. Acknowledge them and then let them wander right back out of your mind. You can help them move along by focusing on the events you've already written about or thinking about other pleasant happenings. You can also have a conversation in your mind with your higher power—just make sure it's centered on thanks, instead of asking for something.

# MOON RITUALS

Since ancient times, the moon has been recognized as a powerful source of energy. Different civilizations have called the moon by different names and developed rituals to draw on lunar power, depending on their wants and needs. Let's talk a little bit about the main moon phases and which of them to use for various sleep rituals.

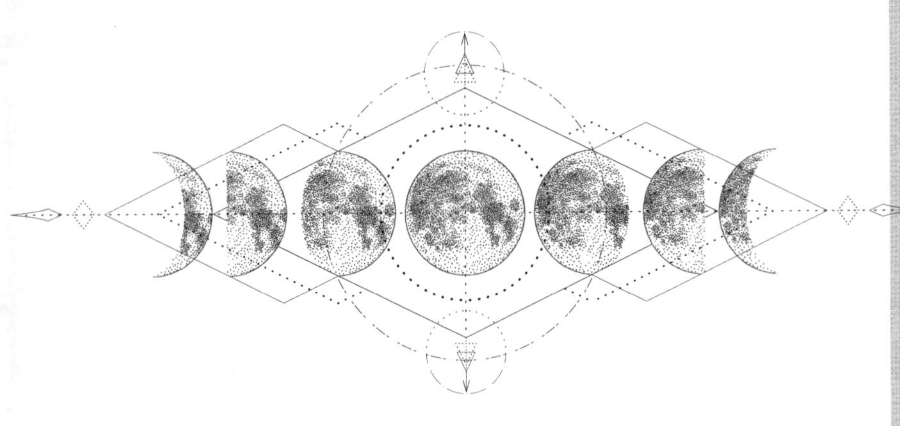

**NEW MOON** This is also sometimes called the "dark moon," when the moon is not visible in the sky; hence, the night sky is pitch black, and if you happen to be outside you can't see your hands in front of your face. This is the best time to use the moon for your sleep spells or rituals, as it's a time of quiet energy, useful for rest and reflection.

**WAXING MOON** The moon's size appears to increase in the days leading up to the full moon. This phase is a time to think about growth in your life. What are the things you would like to improve upon or bring to fruition?

If the answer happens to be rest and relaxation, this is a good time to set an intention for that purpose.

**FULL MOON** The full moon is a time of high energy, elevated emotion, and increased illumination of the night sky. It's natural that some people report difficulty sleeping during this phase so it's a good idea to spend more time meditating now to promote better sleep.

**WANING MOON** As the full moon fades, the moon appears to decrease in size. During this phase, you should focus on anything you want to remove from or decrease in your life. If you'd like to decrease the amount of stress you have so that you can improve your sleep, this would be a good time to focus on diminishing tension and anxiety levels.

November is a particularly good time to use the moon to bring about peacefulness. During this time, the Snow Moon promotes tranquility and contemplation.

If it's possible, go outside and bathe yourself in the light (or dark) of the moon's energy before you go to bed. This is relatively easy if you live in a temperate climate, but more difficult if it's freezing. (Most people don't find it comfortable or relaxing to be outside at night in the dead of winter!) If this is the case, go ahead and perform your ritual near a window—you're still using the moon's light, and you are keeping yourself warm and cozy, which will help to promote a good night's rest.

For the ritual itself, try one or more of the spells that follow.

# Crystal Moon Sleep Spell

There are various crystal energies that help to decrease chaos and confusion and bring about serenity. This ritual combines this soothing crystal energy with the moon's magick to help you sleep soundly and well. For best results, place your stone(s) in direct moonlight for several nights leading up to your ritual. This will "charge" them by allowing them to absorb lunar energy. You can use a single crystal or several types in combination.

## MATERIALS

1 or more of the following stones:

- Amethyst
- Angelite
- Black tourmaline
- Blue lace agate
- Celestite
- Fluorite
- Lepidolite

## RITUAL

Set your intention. Sit quietly in the lunar glow, bring your hands to your chest, and feel your heart beating. Take several deep breaths and feel the rhythm of your heart becoming slower. Inhale through your nose; exhale through your mouth. Say aloud:

*"Bring peace to my heart and soul*
*so that I may have a restful sleep tonight."*

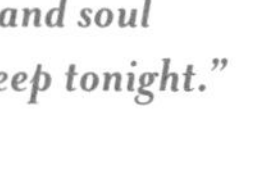

If you are using a single crystal, first assess your chakras (discussed in chapter 3). Where are you feeling tension? What is preventing you from sleeping well? If, for example, you feel as though you aren't being heard or understood, place the crystal on your throat chakra.

If you are using multiple crystals, create a force field of sorts by outlining a circle that is large enough for you to sit or lie in. Place the crystals along the edges of this outline. You don't have to have enough crystals to make an entire outline, just enough to follow the general shape of the force field (you can do this with just four or five stones).

As you sit, either in your force field or with a crystal balancing a chakra, breathe deeply and invite peace into your being. Know that worrisome thoughts may continue to linger on the edge of your mind, and this is normal. Let them stay on the periphery until the morning comes. You may even want to say out loud, "This is not the time for these thoughts. I will give them some time tomorrow." In this practice, you are not trying to force anxiety from your mind altogether (which is often impossible); you are simply saying that each set of thoughts has an appropriate time and place—and nighttime is reserved for a positive mind-set only!

## Moonlight Yoga Poses

Try some restorative yoga poses under the soothing light of the moon, which will amplify the relaxing aspect of the poses. You can do these exercises during any phase of the moon. (*Note:* These are very basic poses but, as with any exercise program, it is best to consult with your health-care practitioner first.)

## Easy Pose

- **Sit on the ground** or a mat and stretch your legs out straight in front of you.
- **Bend your left leg,** tucking your left foot under your right leg.
- **Bend your right leg** and tuck your right foot under your left leg.
- **Sit up straight,** feeling your tailbone tucking underneath you.
- **Place one hand** on each knee.
- **Breathe deeply** and focus on your intention.

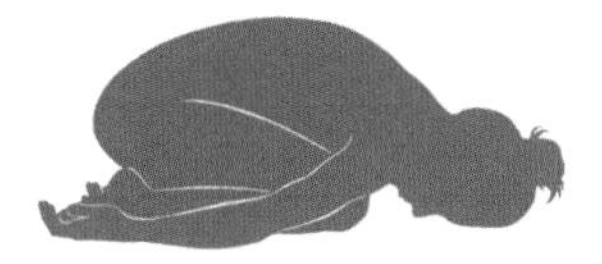

## Child's Pose

- **Kneel on the ground** with your big toes touching each other. Sit back on your heels and then open up your legs about hip-width.
- **Exhale and lean forward,** bringing your torso down between your knees.

- **Reach your hands** back toward your feet, with your palms up, and let your shoulders drop toward the floor.
- **Breathe deeply,** inhaling through your nose and exhaling through your mouth.

## Happy Baby Pose

- **Lie on your back** on the ground or on a mat. Bend your knees and pull them up to your stomach.
- **Grab the outsides of your feet.** Open up this pose so that your knees are just a bit wider than your torso, and then pull your feet toward your armpits.
- **Relax. Breathe.** Focus on welcoming serenity into your heart and mind.

## Corpse Pose

- **Sit on the ground or on a mat.** The goal of this pose is to put your entire body into a neutral state, so even though it looks like you're just lying on the ground, getting to this pose takes some effort!
- **Bend your legs,** and then lean back on your elbows and forearms. Inhale and then, with intention, stretch your right leg all the way

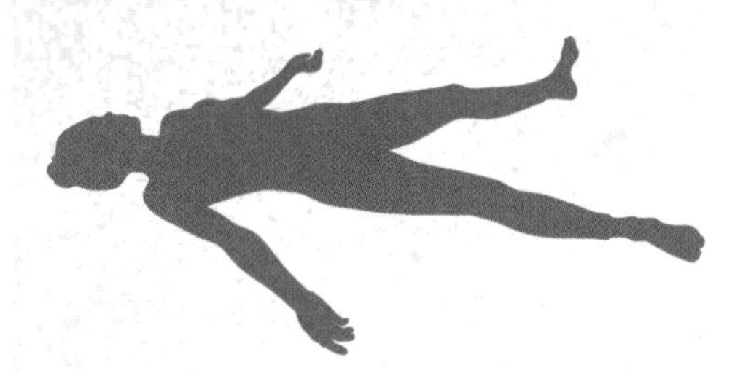

out. Do the same thing with your left leg. Lift up on both heels, and then settle your pelvis into a neutral position. Let your feet fall open.

- **Lower yourself** so that you're lying flat on the ground. With both hands, reach up to the base of your skull and glide your fingers up on it slightly, very gently loosening it from the immediate area of your neck and back. (Take extra care not to pull or tug; the neck is a very sensitive area of the body.) Feel your neck relax. Shake your head from side to side once or twice, to further relax the muscles.
- **Reach both arms up to the sky.** As you bring them down, feel each shoulder blade settle onto the mat or ground. Breathe into the space between your shoulder blades so that the area seems to expand.
- **Continue to breathe deeply,** inviting the soothing moon energy to wash over you.

The goal of each of these poses is to start your body and mind on a nightlong journey of relaxation. As with any type of practice, it comes down to trial and error and finding out what works best for you. Have some fun with these poses and design your own modifications and/or combinations of practices!

Happy dreaming!

## Chapter 5

# Listen Up! Sound Therapy Heals the Soul

MOST OF US TAKE SOUND FOR GRANTED—THE NOISES surrounding us every day. Sounds can soothe or annoy us, but either way, they have a definite effect on our emotional and physical health.

Sound is one of those things that can transport us to a different time and place instantly, which is why many witches like to play meditative music while spellcasting. Chanting and drumming are regularly used in spiritual ceremonies. Some groups perform spiritual "gong baths" in the forest, which are meant to cleanse energies as well. A song, a voice, sounds of nature—all these things can connect us with emotions of happiness, inspiration, peace, or even melancholy.

Every sound has a specific vibration, but there are also very low vibrations that we can't hear but that can still be detected by the body and manifest as anxiety or irritation. Extremely low frequency sound waves—which can cause disruption of neurological functions in humans—have even been explored by some governments, in what are known as microwave arms. Today, some countries use a Mosquito alarm to break up crowds of disruptive young people. It emits a sound at a high frequency that can only be heard by those under the age of twenty-five (and as the name implies, its noise is an irritant)!

Thankfully, sound can be used for healing and empowerment as well. Think about some of your favorite sounds:

- Ocean waves
- A cat purring
- Birds in the springtime
- Crickets at dusk
- Your favorite music

Each of these may have a different effect on your mood, but they are all positive. When a sound is particularly pleasant or soothing to us, we identify with its flow or rhythm. A calm comes over us, our own rhythm—our heartbeat—slows down, and our entire mood shifts. Think about a baby being soothed by a lullaby or the sound of their mother's voice. That instinct doesn't change as we get older—we just find other sounds comforting.

The world around us is influenced by sound energy. Different animals respond positively to various types of music—for example, the BBC reported that sea lions like R&B, while cows and crocodiles react well to classical music.

Studies have shown that birdsong and bee buzzing actually stimulate plant growth! Although not scientifically proven, many people claim that plants also respond to soothing human sounds, like voices or calming music.

## SOUL-SOOTHING SOUNDS

There are sounds and hums that are particularly helpful for soothing our spiritual and emotional energy. Anxiety, stress, and depression can be reduced or managed quite effectively by sound.

### Singing Bowls

Typically called Himalayan singing bowls, these meditation aids are often made from a mix of seven metals (generally copper, gold, or brass; iron; lead; mercury; silver; tin; and zinc) and produce vibrations and sounds meant to restore out-of-balance energies. Sound is produced by rolling a mallet around the rim of the bowl. Their tones have been shown to do the following:

- Reduce anxiety and stress
- Lower blood pressure and heart rate
- Improve focus and intuition
- Promote deep relaxation

You can also use a singing bowl to cleanse the energy of a space or a person with these techniques:

- **To cleanse the energy of your home or another space,** hold the bowl on a small cushion in your left hand, and walk around the area in a clockwise direction, rolling the mallet on the bowl. You can end this ritual by placing the bowl on a table in the center of the space and ringing it there.
- **To cleanse your own energy,** stand outdoors in the sunlight. You can either hold the bowl or place it on a surface in front of you. Circle the bowl with the mallet. Imagine the positive energy flowing around you and taking hold, while it carries away negative energy.

Use a singing bowl for cleansing after you've had an argument with a loved one, when you move into a new home, after an illness, or whenever you feel stuck or in a rut.

### Crystal Singing Bowls

These are similar in appearance to singing bowls but are made from crystal (usually quartz), although sometimes they're composed of a blend of other stones as well. Yogis often start and end their classes with these bowls. The theory is that crystal bowls resonate better with the human body than metal ones do because of the crystalline structure of our teeth and bones. As with metal bowls, sound is produced by rolling a mallet.

Crystal bowls offer many of the same benefits as metal bowls. In addition, because crystal bowls produce sounds that match the vibrations of the chakras, they are ideal for chakra balancing and cleansing. For reference, the corresponding notes of the chakras are:

**ROOT CHAKRA:** C

**SACRAL CHAKRA:** D

**SOLAR PLEXUS CHAKRA:** E

**HEART CHAKRA:** F

**THROAT CHAKRA:** G

**THIRD-EYE CHAKRA:** A

**CROWN CHAKRA:** B

If you don't have a crystal singing bowl handy, you might try balancing your chakras with another instrument using these same notes.

Chakras also respond to certain tones, so try placing your hands over the area of the chakra indicated, and exhale fully, making the following sounds:

**ROOT CHAKRA:** Uhh

**SACRAL CHAKRA:** Ooh

**SOLAR PLEXUS CHAKRA:** Aww

**HEART CHAKRA:** Ahh

**THROAT CHAKRA:** Ayy

**THIRD-EYE CHAKRA:** Aye

**CROWN CHAKRA:** Om

Repeat several times as your hands move over at each chakra point, and feel each chakra vibrate with your exhalation.

# Create Your Own Rituals

The next time you cast a spell, why not play some New Age or meditation music? Throughout our spellcasting years, we have found that playing music while performing rituals helps to strengthen the intent of a spell. It infiltrates the magick, making spells more meaningful—and with that comes power. You might prefer to bang a drum or ring some prayer bells to mark the beginning of the ceremony and repeat again once the spell is over to close down the ritual.

Every practice discussed in this book is meant to give you ideas and a spark of creativity for taking care of your mind, body, and spirit. Make sure to incorporate aspects of rituals that speak to you and create a loving and accepting space for spiritual growth. Setting intention, using meditation or prayer, arranging a crystal field, soaking in the sunlight or moonlight, running a warm bath by candlelight—all these things can enhance your practice. Sometimes you will learn what works by trial and error, but when you do establish your own ceremonies, stick with them. Put the time and effort into your physical and psychic self—you are more than worth it. You are priceless!

## CASTING SPELLS TO MUSIC

Researchers are studying how certain sounds, such as music, beneficially stimulate the vagus nerve, our longest and most complex cranial nerve. The vagus nerve extends from the brain stem down to the intestines, branching out to the heart, lungs, abdomen, and more. Positively stimulating the vagus nerve can reduce stress, benefiting your entire nervous system. Research has shown that music helps to alleviate depression and pain in post-surgical patients. Likewise, when you incorporate soothing sounds into your rituals, you're launching your intentions into the ether from a solid and steady base.

You don't have to stream orchestral music to get the benefits. Think back to when witchcraft was first practiced, usually outside. Witches during that time played whatever instruments they had on hand, usually a drum or sticks that they beat in a rhythmic pattern, building in intensity. Witches used chants to call upon spirits for assistance, or to focus and clarify their intentions. They called on other witches to join their circle for community and support, and the music and dancing took on an even larger role in the ritual.

To carry that same energy over into today's modern spellcasting, get creative! If you already know how to play an instrument, think about how you can incorporate it into your rituals. For example, the flute is an extremely portable instrument that you could take anywhere—but what if you play the piano? You could bring a smaller portable keyboard when casting a spell in the woods, or you might want to do your spellcasting indoors—sitting down at the piano either to play during a ritual or to compose a song that you can hum during your outdoor rituals. Or you might record yourself and play the recording wherever you happen to be. Alternatively, you could play to relax your mind and spirit before casting a spell.

Singing and chanting are also simple ways of bringing beautiful and powerful sound to your ritual. You can sing or chant loudly or softly no matter where you happen to be: in your home, in your car, in the bathtub, in the forest. You don't even have to make up the words yourself; if you find a quote or lyric or poem that speaks to you, simply set it to your own tune or rhythm and carry on from there.

Before you can create or receive anything from your magick or the Universe, you need to believe that you are deserving. Always approach a spell with confidence and a belief that your ritual will work. So often, witches become plagued with self-doubt, which leads to a poor end result. Most of the magick stems from the power of your mind and what you project outward. Just as when you tackle any practical problem in life, the more confident you are, the greater your achievement will be. The basis for all of this is being grounded and open to all kinds of possibilities.

For example, if you are casting a spell to bring your own power into reality, try chanting the words: "*If it's to be, it's up to me.*" Repeat this chant over and over again. Now get up and add a little rhythmic step to your chant. If you have a handheld drum, use it. Focus on what you're saying and believe it. Feel it. Know that it's the truth! You've brought this simple little line to life with a little movement and rhythm.

## PERSONALITY TYPES: WHO ARE YOU?

Here is a section that explores several different personality types, the kinds of stress each one is prone to, and what sort of sound practice is beneficial to each. There is some crossover between personality types, so you might want to experiment with which sounds work best for you. Performing a daily mantra, accompanied by a healing sound (that's either live or played from an online source), usually in the morning when you wake up, helps to drum up the magick throughout the rest of the day. For those who have extreme symptoms, repeat the chant and sound therapy periodically through the day or whenever you feel that you are overwhelmed. There are no hard-and-fast rules; you might want to simply speak or chant the mantra once, but, if you prefer, you can repeat it over and over again until your mood has lifted. You can also play the sounds on their own if you are feeling particularly stressed. (*Note:* Ongoing symptoms of anxiety and depression might be symptomatic of deeper issues for which you should consult a therapist or health-care professional.)

## The Worrier

Everyone worries about something, at least once in a while, but sometimes you can lose all sense of perspective, exacerbating the stress. Once someone falls into a pattern of excessive worry, that can be a difficult habit to break; the worrier tends to imagine the worst-case scenario all the time. Worriers can benefit from mindfulness exercises, keeping themselves grounded in the moment, and giving themselves reminders that they are safe.

**CRYSTAL TO CARRY:** Moonstone (hold or wear as jewelry)

**MANTRA:** *"Fears will leave me, it shall be, relaxed, calm, and worry free."*

**SOUND** Bell

## The Stressed-Out

This person tends to take on project after project, either because they are an overachiever, or because they feel as though they can't say no. They may be a phenomenal organizer and worker bee, but eventually things pile up and they blow a gasket. Some of these folks turn to drugs or alcohol to self-medicate, but they would do particularly well with deep breathing, meditation, and relaxation practices.

**CRYSTAL TO CARRY:** Hematite

**MANTRA:** *"Tranquil mind, remove my frown, at last my mood will settle down."*

**SOUND:** Ocean waves

## The Flustered

While the worrier is focused on negative outcomes, people who are easily flustered are often prone to nervousness or fear, not prompted by a particular reason. Often these people have an excess of adrenaline pumping through their veins and can benefit from channeling their nervous energy into exercising, whether running, weight lifting, or yoga.

**CRYSTAL TO CARRY:** Amber

**MANTRA:** *"Pent up power, I dispel, with calm of mind, this day goes well."*

**SOUND:** Birdsong

## The Perfectionist

The perfectionist can be very exacting and will constantly set challenges for themselves, not being able to settle unless everything around them is just right. This can sometimes lead to them setting unrealistic goals and when they fall short of those goals, they may feel consumed by a fear of failure.

**CRYSTAL TO CARRY:** Rose quartz

**MANTRA:** *"If I fail then so it will be, for I'm not perfect, this is me."*

**SOUND:** Rain

## The Self-Doubter

Low self-esteem and worry combine in this personality type to cause a constant stream of second-guessing and self-criticism. This is a person who always feels as though they've made the wrong choice, even when the decision at hand is minor. The self-doubter does well with meditation and mantras that remind them that their opinions have value.

**CRYSTAL TO CARRY:** Carnelian

**MANTRA:** *"I am my best, I shall succeed, with all I do, my doubts are freed."*

**SOUND:** Whale song

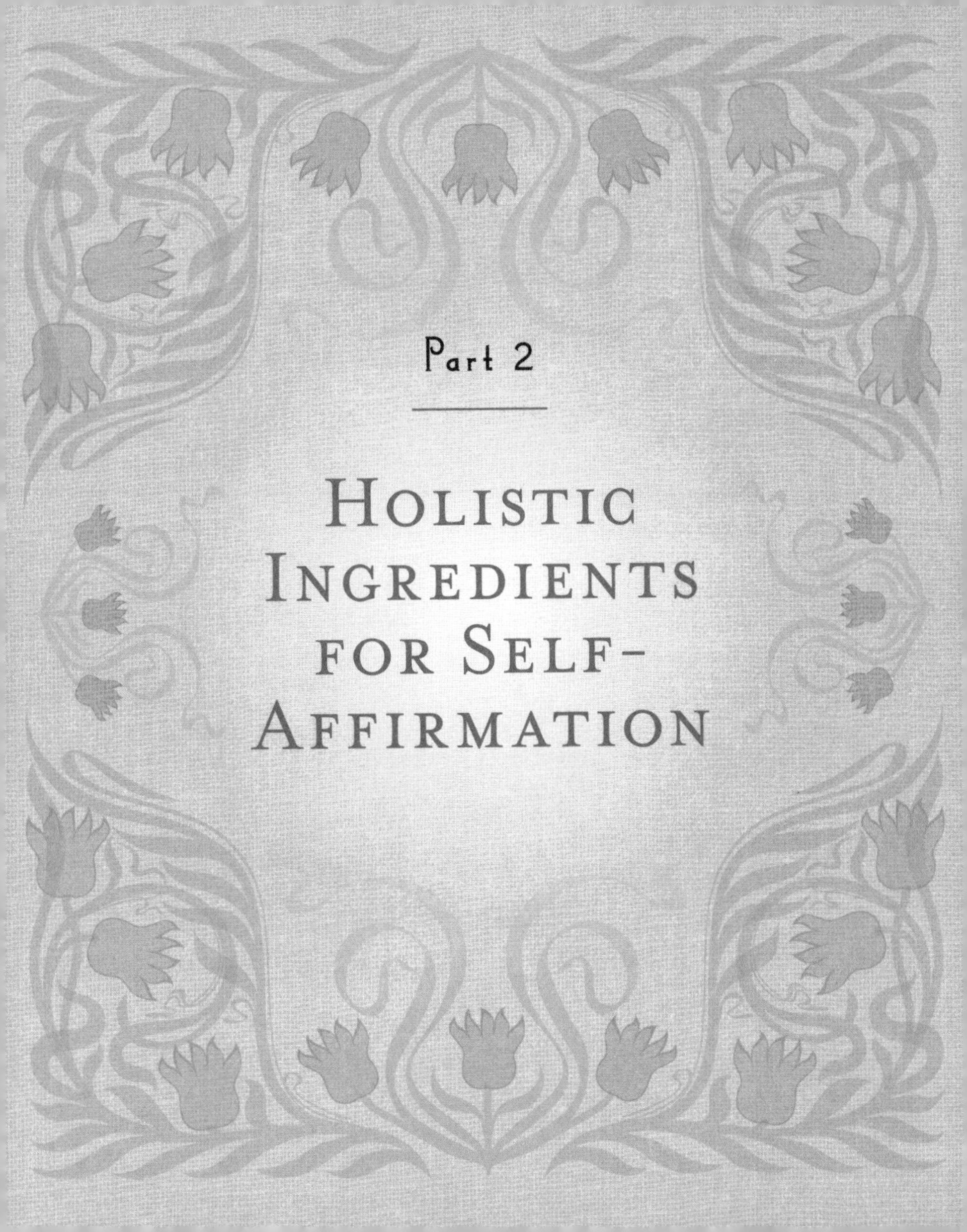

Part 2

# Holistic Ingredients for Self-Affirmation

# Chapter 6

# Must-Have Herbs for Witches

LONG BEFORE HUMANS GRACED THE EARTH WITH their footsteps, forests and flora blossomed and grew, unencumbered by borders, construction, or other human-made obstacles.

The ancient Greek philosopher Aristotle said that plants did far more than just provide basic nutrition; he suggested that they possessed a soul. Modern science has found that plants communicate with each other through an underground network of roots and fungi, and also by releasing chemicals into the air. If a plant has been attacked by malicious insects—such as aphids—it releases defensive chemicals that will repel the aphids and attract the aphids' natural predator, wasps. Amazingly, other plants in the same fungal network have been found to also release the same chemicals, even if they are not under attack! We have to honor our planet and realize that Mother Nature is far more complex than we can even begin to understand. Even as our world continues to be littered and besmirched with plastics and pollution, she finds a way to restore and repair as best as she can. When you're in the woods or out in nature, you are truly not alone. There's an entire ecosystem surrounding you with constant chatter and energy.

Some witches like to grow their own herbs, and if that's possible for you to do, there is no better way to gain a deeper connection to the materials you're using in your spells. There's something magickally satisfying about taking a seed and pushing it into the soil, only to watch it develop and grow into a full-size plant. During its young life and while you tend to it, you are exchanging your energy with it—so by the time it reaches full maturity, you will develop a bond that is unique to you both. This relationship enhances any magick you practice in the future, so, in a way, it's best to have a go at growing your own. For some herbs, you don't even need a garden: a windowsill or a small patio will do just fine. Of course, if you are lucky enough to have a plot of land, you can grow much more and experiment with plants that are not readily available.

If you don't have a green-thumb or you live in a climate where it's not possible to cultivate plants, there are oodles of witches who sell their surplus herbs online. These people will have grown their plants with the same positive intent that you might have done if you'd grown them yourself. What's most important is to dig deep and learn about the plants you're working with, and then choose them deliberately, based on your intention and needs.

Botanists have a precise definition of what constitutes an "herb" as opposed to a "plant" or a "fungus." Wiccans use the words a little differently. When we talk about herbal medicine or herbology, we're speaking about using all-natural sources of healing to promote well-being. Almost every plant on earth possesses healing or magickal properties, and I'm sure that witches would like to include them all in their rituals. For now, though, we will be covering the most commonly used herbs a witch might have on hand, with examples of how to use them magickally in your everyday lives. (*Note:* We will not be covering herbal healing here, as that is the subject of a book in itself! Also, many herbs may interact with numerous medications and/or be contraindicated for pregnancy, breastfeeding, and certain medical conditions, so it is best to discuss using herbs for medicinal purposes with your health-care practitioner.)

## ALOE VERA (*Aloe vera*)

Aloe vera has been in steady use as a skin healing agent since Cleopatra's time; it is said that she relied on aloe to maintain her youthful beauty. In ancient Egypt it was called the "plant of eternity," and because of its antibacterial and antifungal properties, it was used to embalm the dead.

Aloe is originally from the Middle East, but grows widely around the world. It is readily available in most plant shops and is best to grow indoors, needing minimal watering.

## Magickal Properties

- In Africa, aloe is hung in baskets around the home to bring good fortune to the family and to protect against evil and accidents.
- In Mexico, it is added to special wreaths that are hung for good luck and wealth.

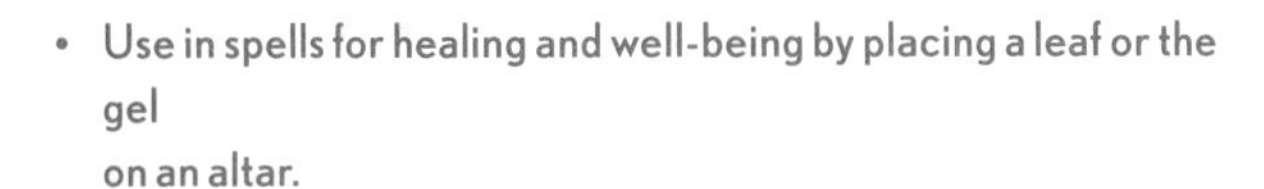

- Use in spells for healing and well-being by placing a leaf or the gel on an altar.
- Use for magickal beauty balms.
- For prophetic dreams and astral projection, sleep with an aloe leaf by your bed.
- Used in most spells for protection and healing.

## Aloe Vera Face Cream Ritual

You can create your own aloe-themed ritual for relaxation, protection, and self-care with an aloe vera cream.

**MATERIALS**

1 good-sized aloe vera leaf

A sharp knife

A small spoon

A small bowl

1 teaspoon mineral oil

A few drops of lavender or frankincense essential oil, for fragrance*

A few drops of vitamin E oil (optional)

A blender**

A glass jar

## RITUAL

Cut the aloe vera leaf open and use a spoon to scoop out the gel and transfer it to a bowl.

Add the mineral oil and the fragrant essential oil (and, if desired, the vitamin E oil). Mix the gel and oil in a blender until creamy. Strain the mixture through a sieve to make sure there are no lumps before transferring it to a small glass jar.

Test a small patch on your skin, cover with a bandage, and wait 24 hours to make sure you do not have any skin reactions. If the skin patch test is fine, stand in front of the mirror each morning and apply a few dabs of the cream to your face. While massaging it into your skin, say this chant repeatedly until you are finished applying the cream:

*"Aloe vera remove my stress, my skin is now renewed and fresh."*

Let it sit for a moment while you visualize a white light of protection and healing around you.

*Lavender has contraindications in boys relating to hormonal interactions; it is also not advisable to use it if you're pregnant or breastfeeding, as not enough is known about the interactions, and it can slow down the central nervous system, so it should be avoided before surgery.

**The blender you use for this ritual and others should not be used for food, only for magickal mixing.

## ARNICA (*Arnica montana*)

Arnica is a bright yellow flower in the sunflower family that looks similar to a daisy; it grows in northwest North America and northern Asia and Europe. It has many different popular names, including mountain tobacco, leopard's bane, and wolfsbane (the latter two are also common names for an unrelated genus of plant, *Aconitum*). Arnica can be poisonous if ingested, and can cause skin irritation (and can be absorbed by the skin), so take care when handling it.

### Magickal Properties

- Associated with Midsummer and the goddess Freya, so use this time to show gratitude to the sun. Get up early in the morning to watch the sun rise and, in your own words, thank the sun for sending light to the earth.
- Used in spells for fertility and childbirth.
- Aids in spells to diminish thunderstorms, blizzards, and snowstorms.
- Repels evil spirits in the home.
- Keeps enemies from crossing your threshold.
- Dry the leaves in the sun and sprinkle them around the entrances of your home for protection.

# BASIL (*Ocimum*)

If you like to cook, chances are you already know a lot about basil. It's easy to find and not difficult to grow; however, there are different types. With more than one hundred varieties of basil, sweet basil—the kind you're likely to come across in the store—is probably the most common. It can be used in most spells, but you can also use the hardier variety, holy basil, which is popular, too.

**SWEET BASIL** *(Ocimum basilicum)* Native to India and tropical Asia, this herb possesses a wealth of medicinal and magickal properties. Throughout the world today, it is more commonly used in recipes, but it's not just delicious in tomato sauce; it's a fabulously powerful plant that contains great power.

## Magickal Properties

In days of yore, sweet basil was used to protect people from spells cast by their enemies; today, people still use it to ward off negative energies, usually by scattering fresh or dried leaves around doorways or windows. Sweet basil is often used in love spells, as its pleasant scent promotes good feelings between couples. Italian legend has it that if a man accepts a basil trimming from a lady, they are destined to be together. Try adding this herb to a recipe or place basil trimmings around your home to ensure harmony between you and a loved one.

- Used in spells to inspire a lover to remain faithful, by slipping crushed leaves into a recipe or by using burnt leaves in a ritual.
- For fertility, try hanging a bunch of fresh sweet basil above the bed and making love underneath it during a new moon phase.

## A Basil Spell to Protect Your Business

The worry of owning your own business is sometimes quite overwhelming, especially if your employees are relying on you to pay their wages. If your business is flagging or you simply want to keep the workload ticking along nicely, you can use sweet basil to bless the premises. It's easy—all you have to do is either plant or buy a pot of basil and place it in the window of your business. If you work from home, make sure that there is a pot growing somewhere in the house. Keep the basil watered and free of pests. Alternatively, by carrying a basil leaf in your pocket, it will draw luck and wealth to you.

**HOLY BASIL** *(Ocimum tenuiflorum)* Described as an annual shrub, holy basil is native to the Indian subcontinent. It is a sacred plant in Hinduism, and associated with an avatar of the Hindu goddess Lakshmi, wife of Vishnu, the god who preserves and protects life. Holy basil is worshipped in Hindu rituals, and is often found growing around temples and sacred spaces in India, as well as in the courtyards of Hindu homes.

## Magickal Properties

- Holy basil creates a peaceful vibe and helps to balance the chakras and clear obstacles that may be blocking your energies.
- Possesses a protective quality and is used to ward off evil spirits.
- Invites happiness into life and is used in love magick to attract a mate. On the Friday of a full moon, light a pink candle and take a bath; add a few leaves

to the tub. Concentrate on the kind of partner you might want to attract and imagine yourself and your new love uniting.

- Helps repel negative obstacles and cleanse chakras.

## A Spell to Unblock the Chakras

You'll emerge feeling refreshed and balanced after this ritual; it will loosen any energetic wheels that might be spinning too slowly.

**MATERIALS**

Handful of crushed fresh holy basil leaves

A white candle

A small fireproof bowl

A lighter or matches

**RITUAL**

Scatter about ¾ of the crushed holy basil leaves on the floor in a large circle.

Place the ceremonial white candle in the bowl, place the bowl in the center of the circle, and light the candle. Place the remaining holy basil leaves inside the bowl.

Seat yourself in the center of the circle and start your meditation, focusing on any blockages you may feel in the chakras. Allow yourself to breathe deeply and concentrate on the flow of your spiritual energy. Continue with the meditation for as long as you like.

# BERGAMOT (*Citrus bergamia*)

If you are one of the many folks who just love a spot of tea now and again, you may already be a fan of the bergamot orange—and you probably didn't even know it! The bergamot tree is native to southern Asia and is found growing in abundance in southern Italy as well. It produces a citrus fruit that has a crisp, fresh smell (but a rather bitter taste), and the oil from the peel of the fruit is used to flavor Earl Grey tea.

## Magickal Properties

- Bergamot is particularly good for cleansing the soul of heavy energies, like sadness, worry, and even grief.
- Bergamot helps to reconnect us with our true selves when we're getting too weighed down with negativity. Try putting 10 drops of bergamot oil in your bath and soak until you can feel the dark energy replaced by a lighter force. Make sure to rinse with clean water before you leave the tub. (*NOTE:* Patch-test your skin first for 24 hours before bathing; bergamot oil might make your skin photosensitive, so be sure to rinse well. Do not use bergamot if you're pregnant or breastfeeding.)
- If you're worried about money, place a few drops of bergamot oil in your wallet—or even directly onto your cash—to reap the benefits. If you prefer not to carry cash around, put a few drops of bergamot oil in a diffuser on your work desk or dab a drop on each palm to increase your cash flow.

## CATNIP (*Nepeta cataria*)

If you have a little feline friend or familiar, you know that catnip, or cat-mint, can turn even the calmest kitty into a bundle of pure craziness. Cats love to roll around in catnip leaves and scratch at them until there's almost no trace of the plants left. This herb, indigenous to southeast Europe, the Middle East, and Asia, is not only a pleasure drug for kitties, but has been used for centuries to promote a psychic connection between felines and their owners.

### Magickal Properties

- Catnip brings good luck and positive spiritual energy to your home if you plant it in your yard or hang it on your door.
- If you hold catnip leaves in your hand until they are warm and then hold hands with someone else, that person will be your forever friend, but only if you store the leaves in a safe spot afterward.
- Catnip is also used in love sachets and spells for love and happiness.

### A Catnip Spell to Attract Romance

For love and friendship spells, mix catnip with rose petals for an extra boost. Try this simple spell to attract the partner of your dreams.

### MATERIALS

- A journal or book of shadows
- 1 teaspoon of dried catnip
- 10 rose petals (any color)
- 2 red candles

### RITUAL

First, take the time to write in your journal about the person you'd like to attract. Be specific: What does this person look like? How old are they? What kind of personality does this person have? Imagine yourself happy and in love with your prospective partner. Place your catnip and rose petals in the center of a table. You can put them directly on the table, or in a container of some sort. Light the red candles and recite this chant with intention:

*"May the love I see in my mind walk into my life.*
*May our love last a lifetime and bring fulfillment to us both.*
*So mote it be."*

Repeat this spell three nights in a row, and romance should start to blossom.

## CHAMOMILE, GERMAN
## *(Matricaria chamomilla)*

The flowers of the German chamomile plant look like tiny little daisies—so happy, so fresh. Native to Europe, Asia, and India, this is a plant long associated with relaxation, healthy sleep, and an improved outlook when life gets stressful. You can grow chamomile easily if you have a garden, and the flower heads are used to brew tea; make infusions; or in tinctures, creams, or ointments. For use in magick, chamomile works in a couple of different ways. First, because it helps to calm and soothe the soul, it opens us up to better psychic and spiritual work. While preparing for a ritual of any sort, you can sip a cup of chamomile tea or prepare a bath to remove the negativity that might be clinging to your spirit. (*Note:* German chamomile may exacerbate hormone-sensitive conditions and interact with estrogen pills, sedative medications, warfarin, tamoxifen, and medications that are changed by the liver, such as lovastatin, triazolam, and others.)

## Magickal Properties

- Chamomile can alleviate weariness and remove toxins and negativity. When preparing a bath, add a handful of fresh chamomile flowers, along with a handful of sea salt, to boost positivity and relaxation. Light a white candle for further purification and protection. Inhale positivity and exhale doubt, frustration, and destructive thoughts. Visualize the outcome you want, but keep it filled with love and light.

- Chamomile also attracts wealth and luck. Let's say you're headed to Las Vegas for a weekend of trying your luck. You might want to whip up a chamomile-filled poppet and keep it in your pocket at the casinos. This will attract luck your way.

- Use chamomile to work against external negative forces and spells. Simply sprinkle the dried flowers around your doorway or any other space you want to purify. Place some flowers on your nightstand, for example, if you're having nightmares or you want to combat insomnia. If your boss has it in for you, scatter chamomile around your workstation to ward off their negative energy.

## A Chamomile Poppet to Improve Your Luck

Make one of these for yourself if you need a boost of good luck—or make one for a friend and instead of the word *my* write their name on the paper. It's a nice gift, especially if they've been having a hard time of it.

**MATERIALS**

- A small piece of red, green, or yellow fabric (colors for good luck)
- A pair of scissors
- A sewing needle and red, green, or yellow thread
- A handful of dried chamomile (leaves and flowers)
- A small piece of paper and pen

**RITUAL**

Cut out two circles of fabric, measuring about 4 inches (10 cm) in diameter, and then sew them together, wrong sides facing, leaving about a 1½ inch (4 cm) gap.

Next, turn the circular fabric right-side out and stuff with the dried chamomile. On a piece of paper, write your name and the words Improve my luck. Fold the paper up and place it inside the pouch. Sew up the circle neatly.

To charm your pouch, hold it up to your forehead and close your eyes. For a few minutes, in your mind, send the pouch your positive thoughts and ask it to change your luck for the better. Make sure you carry this lucky pouch with you at all times and pop it under your pillow every night.

## LAVENDER (*Lavendula*)

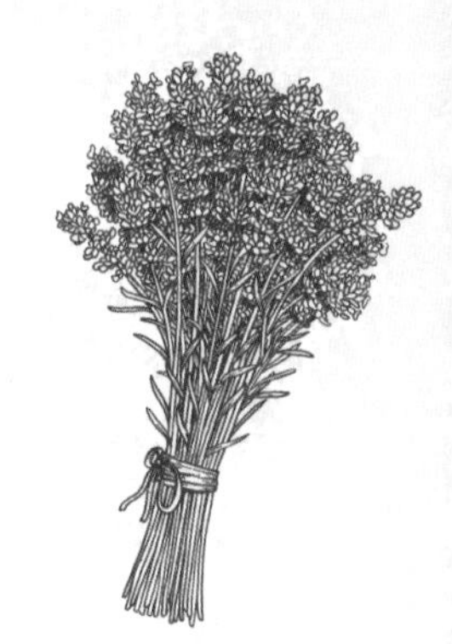

Oftentimes, when you walk into a spa, that lovely scent that greets you is a lavender mix. This herb—native to Europe, eastern Africa, southwest Asia, and India—is hailed as a scent that helps to alleviate anxiety and to encourage relaxation. Today lavender is enjoying a heyday of sorts in our highly stressed world.

### Magickal Properties

- It is believed that lavender will awaken the love of your soul mate and draw them to you. You can spritz yourself with a perfume or dab a drop or two of essential oil on to your pulse points. Adding lavender-infused bath salts to your tub also yields the same effect.
- If things aren't going so well in your current relationship, this herb helps to calm tensions so that love can bloom again.
- If a child or baby is in a cranky mood, the lavender scent can help soothe them, which is why it is sometimes added to baby bath products and creams.
- Used to purify and protect. Place a sprig of lavender in each of the four corners of your home or on the outside walls to prevent negative energies from entering or taking hold. You can also place dried sprigs or fresh plants as decorative touches around your home, and they will have the same effect.
- Bathing in lavender helps to draw out negative energy, which is part of the reason it leaves you feeling relaxed. Just make sure to rinse the tub with clean water when you are done as the tiny petals will be left behind.

## Use Lavender to Keep Bad Dreams at Bay

If you suffer a lot with bad dreams, it might be that when you are sleeping you are, inadvertently, visiting the lower astral planes. This is where some of the lesser entities hang out, so it's imperative that you protect yourself before you go to sleep. One good way is to have a nightly chat with your guide and ask them to keep you safe and away from anything negative. Another more practical way is to purchase a dream catcher; these can be bought quite inexpensively online. Weave some lavender sprigs in and out of your dream catcher and hang it on the wall by your bed. You could also place a few sprigs of lavender inside your pillowcase or combine your nightly ritual with a cup of chamomile tea. It will enhance relaxation and keep you protected at the same time.

## MUGWORT (*Artemisia vulgaris*)

Mugwort has been used for centuries as an important protective herb throughout Europe, Asia, India, and North Africa. Roman soldiers placed mugwort in their sandals to cushion their feet during their long marches, and witches would place a few leaves of mugwort in the soles of their shoes to ensure safety and protection when traveling. It was also worn by medieval revelers on the holiday of St. John's Eve (June 23)—as the herb was associated with John the Baptist—for luck and to protect them from illness.

## Magickal Properties

- Mugwort is one of those herbs that is thought to boost the power of any ritual. By simply placing a dish of dried mugwort on the altar throughout the duration of a spell, you will get a more successful result. Therefore, it's an essential ingredient in any witch's toolbox.
- Used to invoke clairvoyance and improve psychic readings. Also, a dish of mugwort by the bedside is believed to transport the sleeper into the astral plane.
- Rubbing the leaves onto a crystal ball, tarot cards, or a magickal mirror is thought to enhance the Seer's visions.
- Hang dried mugwort in the kitchen for protection.
- Modern-day witches carry on the St. John's Eve tradition on the Wiccan holiday of Litha (Midsummer's Eve) and toss mugwort into the fire as a means of bringing good fortune to themselves during the coming year.
- Make your own magickal anointing oil by steeping a few sprigs of mugwort in 2 tablespoons of pure vegetable oil and leave overnight. This oil will last three months if you transfer it into a small glass bottle with a screw-top lid.

(*NOTE:* Mugwort oil should not be used if you are pregnant or breastfeeding; it also might cause skin allergies so patch-test a small area before use and wait 24 hours.)

## A Mugwort Ritual to Promote Clairvoyance

For psychic individuals who would like to boost their abilities, making a mugwort dream pillow can really clarify your visions.

**MATERIALS**

Handful of dried mugwort leaves

A white cloth handkerchief

A few drops of mugwort essential oil

A sewing needle and white thread

**RITUAL**

Place the dried mugwort in the center of the cloth handkerchief. Sprinkle a few drops of the mugwort essential oil on the herbs, fold the cloth in quarters to form a pouch, and then stitch the edges all the way around until the pouch is sealed.

Place this pouch under your pillow and sleep with it each night. You might also like to recite a little incantation before you close your eyes, something like this:

*"I ask for lucid and peaceful visions as I sleep,*
*and for understanding of the images that come to me.*
*So mote it be."*

## ROSEMARY (*Salvia rosmarinus*)

Rosemary looks a lot like lavender at first glance, but, aromatically, the two plants are quite different. Native to the Mediterranean and an

important ingredient in cuisines of the region, rosemary flowers have a purplish-blue hue. There are various legends linking the color to the Virgin Mary's cloak, but the Latin word *rosmarinus* literally means "dew of the sea."

## Magickal Properties

- Witchy students swear that rosemary works as an aid for concentration and focus. Chewing a few sprigs before exams and tests enhances a person's concentration.
- Used as a smudging herb, to clear and protect people and places from negative energy. You can purchase ready-made smudging sticks easily or, if you grow the plant, make your own by binding a large bunch of rosemary tightly with string.
- Hang rosemary in the windows of your home to ward off jealousy.
- Keep a sprig outside by the front door or plant a bush in the garden to keep a partner faithful.
- Planting this herb by the main entrance to a home is also believed to ward off thieves.
- Eating rosemary regularly helps to dispel grief and anger.
- Infuse rosemary leaves in boiling water and sip as a tea to boost creativity.

## Rosemary Tarot Card Blessing

If you want to cleanse your tarot cards after every reading, a lovely way to do this is to burn rosemary. Light one end of a rosemary sprig with a lighter, immediately blow it out, and place it into a fireproof bowl. Keep a bottle of water nearby. Continue to gently blow on the smoldering sprig so that it produces a smoke that drifts over or nearby your cards. Fan the smoke around the space and over the surface where you will be working. Ask the spirits to cleanse and bless your cards, making them ready for the next time you use them. Take care to then douse the sprig with the water when you are done.

## SAGE (*Salvia Officinalis*)

This potent plant is thought to be the sister herb to rosemary, as they are both from the Mediterranean and grow well when planted side by side. Its benefits have long been associated with longevity, meaning that if it is growing wild in the garden, the owner of the property will live a long and healthy life. Sage is easy to grow, but beware: some witches believe that it's unlucky to plant it in your own garden and advise that someone else plant it for you. We are not too sure about this superstition, but one thing we do encourage: plant two bushes, not one, and luck will always be on your side.

## Magickal Properties

- Write your wishes on a sage leaf and place it under your pillow. If you dream about the wish in the next seventy-two hours, it is said that your wish will come true. If you don't dream of your wish, bury the leaf outside.
- You can use sage in spells and meditations concerning money, career, and home life. Sage attracts luck and wisdom.
- Carry a sage leaf in your pocket or in a locket to guard against evil spirits and hexes.
- Carry sage in your wallet to attract wealth.
- Magickal folklore says that if sage is growing well in a garden, all is well with the family's finances.

## A Sage Spell to Rid a Home of Ghosts

Sage is a spiritual disinfectant, so it is not surprising that one of its most popular uses is to rid anyone or anything of negativity. Shamans teach us that this powerful herb can also banish unwanted spirits. If you think your home is haunted or you get an uneasy feeling when you are on your own, one sure way to keep your house free of spirits is to use a sage smudger. You can purchase dried sage smudging sticks from most New Age shops or you can pick your own homegrown sage and bind it tightly with string. This bundle must be hung in the home until it is completely dried. Once ready, simply light the end of the sage and immediately blow out any flames. You will see the embers smoldering away, leaving behind a pungent smell. With your hand or a feather, waft the smoke around each room in the house.

(*NOTE:* Keep a pot of water handy as you are doing this, and avoid going near flammable surfaces.) You can also boil sage leaves on your stove or light dried leaves in a bowl for a similar effect.

## TARRAGON (*Artemisia dracunculus*)

Tarragon is quite aromatic when growing in the garden—it grows wild throughout the Northern Hemisphere—but when added to dishes, its taste is rather mild and similar to anise. *Dracunculus* is Latin for "little dragon," and in days of yore it was said that tarragon repelled dragons, snakes, and other venomous creatures—if, by chance, you were bitten by a snake, tarragon would heal the bite. And if you were actually out hunting for dragons or other beasts, you might tuck tarragon into your pocket for good luck. Modern-day kitchen witches see tarragon as an essential ingredient to have on hand for many practical and magickal uses.

### Magickal Properties

- Used for centuries to induce tranquility in the home; can be used in spells and charms for peace, compassion, and calming. Put a piece of dried tarragon into a locket or amulet to maintain or bring about harmony, especially if you're in the middle of a chaotic situation.
- Used in love spells or ceremonies to attract love.
- Consecrates sacred altar items. Burn dried tarragon to disinfect your altar.

- Sleeping with tarragon or eating a tarragon leaf before bedtime can bring about lucid dreaming and astral travel.
- Dried and hung tarragon protects the home from evil or disruption.
- Plant tarragon in the garden to help deal with grief when a loved one passes over.
- Used in pouches and poppets to make desires and wishes come true.
- Helps banish anything unwanted from your life.

## A Tarragon Spell to Cast Out Unwanted Situations

Tarragon is wonderful if you want to cast out negative energies. You might be experiencing problems at work or difficult people, even toxic relationships. Write down on a piece of paper the person or thing that you want to be done with. Sit in front of a fire and toss a sprig of tarragon into the fire, along with the piece of paper. Say out loud these words:

*"These written words be gone,*
*With the magickal aid of tarragon.*
*So mote it be."*

If you don't have a fireplace or a firepit, you can place the paper and the herb in a fireproof dish. Either way, the tarragon works to seal in the wish or intent and to start you on a new path.

# THYME (*Thymus*)

Thyme is a little herb that has about a hundred uses, both practical and magickal. Indigenous to the Mediterranean, thyme also cleans things out on the spiritual plane. The ancient Greeks burned thyme in their temples to prepare and purify the spaces for rituals. You can easily carry on this tradition before your own ceremonies, meditation, or spellwork.

## Magickal Properties

- Thyme is especially useful in love spells and charms. To make yourself appealing to the opposite sex, tuck a sprig of fresh thyme behind your ear.
- Tuck a sprig of thyme into dream pillows to prevent nightmares and to increase psychic awareness.
- To draw fairies and elves to your yard, line your garden beds with thyme plants.
- Here's a little divination trick to see the face of your true love: Put thyme in one shoe and rosemary in the other. Sprinkle each shoe with three drops of water, then set them aside for the night. When you are settling into bed, take a moment to call upon your spirit guides to bring you dreams of the person you are meant to be with.

# A Thyme Spell to Give Courage

Simply smelling thyme gives you protection and courage to conquer whatever obstacles your day may bring. But you can take this one step further and prepare yourself a ritual bath, for that will wash away fear and doubt and replace them with bravery and confidence.

## MATERIALS

A white candle

A red candle

5–10 drops of thyme essential oil*

5 drops of rosemary essential oil*

## RITUAL

Draw yourself a warm bath. Near the tub, light the white candle, symbolic of purity; and then light the red candle, to bring out your inner valor.

Place 5–10 drops of thyme essential oil into the water. Add 5 drops of rosemary essential oil. As you stir the bathwater and the oils, speak your spell:

*"Let my heart be like a lion's and let my fears be gone;*
*Let my soul be clear and let my mind be strong.*
*So mote it be."*

*Patch-test your skin for 24 hours with a drop of each of the oils to make sure you have no skin allergies and then bathe in the tub for around 20 minutes. When you have finished, blow out the candles and rinse out the tub.

## VALERIAN (*Aleriana officinalis*)

Valerian is sometimes called "nature's valium" or "all-heal" due to its ability to calm even the most frayed nerves. Native to Europe and parts of Asia, it has a very earthy and root-like smell, which some people find too strong or even unpleasant, but its ability to treat insomnia and quell hyperactivity are almost unmatched in the herbal world. (*Note:* Speak to your health-care practitioner before taking valerian; it causes sleepiness, interacts with many medications, and should not be taken if you're pregnant or breastfeeding, or if you have a planned surgery.)

Some people use valerian as "graveyard dust" in black magic, which means they call upon dark spirits to do their dirty work for them, bringing hexes against their enemies. Remember the rule of Wicca: whatever you put out comes back threefold to you, so harm none!

### Magickal Properties

- Keeping fresh valerian in the home helps to ward off evil spirits and lightning strikes.
- Helps to soothe tensions between couples who are fighting.
- Wearing a sprig of valerian or placing it into a love sachet will attract true love.
- Burning valerian powder, oil, or incense attracts animal spirits.
- Valerian has cleansing energy and can be used to purify your home or your ritual space.

- If you feel that you've picked up some negative vibes, you can put a few drops of valerian oil into your bath and soak for 15–20 minutes. Imagine the negative energy washing away and your strongest, purest energy taking root instead. When you are done soaking, make sure you rinse off with clean water.

## A Valerian Spell to Stop Arguments with Loved Ones

It's never nice when fights occur with someone you live with. This spell will help you both to get past the rows and start to connect again in a more positive way. For this spell you will need to snip a lock of hair from you and from the person you are fighting with; perform the spell on the night of a full moon.

### MATERIALS

2 locks of hair—1 from you and 1 from the person you are arguing with

A dish

1 teaspoon of dried valerian root

A white candle

### RITUAL

Mix the locks of hair together in the dish on a full moon.

Scatter a teaspoon of dried valerian into the bowl and light a white candle. Say this chant 13 times:

*"Stop our quarreling; disputes will end,*
*Smooth the way and let us be friends."*

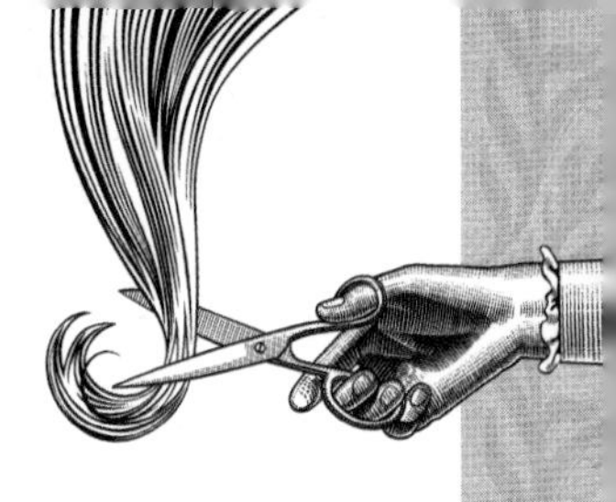

When you have recited the spell 13 times, close the ritual by saying the words *"So mote it be."* Let the candle burn down (never leave a candle unattended—use a tealight, if needed), and then toss the contents of the bowl outside. When it blows away on the wind, the arguments should stop.

## VERVAIN (*Verbena*)

These flowering plants are native to the Americas, Europe. and Asia. It is said that the Romans used vervain to cleanse and decorate their altars and that the Druids wove vervain crowns during initiation rites. The Persians worked it into their sun-worshipping ceremonies, which makes perfect sense, as the plant is most magickally potent when it's harvested during the Summer Solstice or later, during the "dog days" of summer when Sirius, the Dog Star, is on the rise.

Since the beginning of magickal history, vervain has been a mainstay in every witch's and sorcerer's toolbox. Its uses in magick are wide and varied.

### Magickal Properties

- A crown made of vervain protects you during conjuring and other spells.
- Carrying a sprig of vervain provides protection from harm and accidents.
- Vervain placed in your home guards it against lightning strikes.
- An infusion sprinkled around your home keeps negative energies out and purifies the area.

- Soaking in a bath with a few drops of vervain essential oil helps to draw out dark energy from your aura or spirit, can improve your psychic vision, and bring enemies around to your way of thinking. (Do a 24-hour patch test first to make sure it does not cause skin allergies.)
- Vervain brings peace to tense situations and relationships.
- To attract wealth and success, use the herb in a spell for money or plant it near your home.
- Tucking a leaf under your pillow protects you from nightmares.
- Putting vervain under your baby's crib mattress will ensure that he or she will be a bright and sunny child.

## A Vervain Spell to Make Someone Notice You

This herb is used regularly in love potions and spells. For example, you can burn vervain to make the object of your affection take notice of you. Simply place a dried sprig in a fireproof container, visualize the face of the one you love, and then light it with a match or lighter. Say this chant three times:

> ***"In this moment I do see, the love that will belong to me.***
> ***Meld two spirits into one, and with this spell may it be done."***

Once you have recited the spell, close by saying the words, *"So mote it be."*

# YARROW (*Achillea millefolium*)

Yarrow is a lovely little white flower, native to Europe, North America, and western Asia, and can often be found growing wild in meadows and alongside the road. It is also a must-have for a magickal garden, as it has a multitude of uses, both in healing and in divination. Yarrow grows well in a sunny spot and comes back year after year.

## Magickal Properties

- Place yarrow leaves on the altar when conducting love rituals to draw true love near.
- Newlyweds are encouraged to hang dried yarrow in their home to bring seven years of harmony to their budding marriage. You don't have to be a brand-new husband or wife to use this little relationship enhancer, though! Try yarrow to strengthen the bonds of your happy home.
- When carried in an amulet or pouch, yarrow protects from dark energies and gives courage to anyone who carries a bundle in their hand. (In Greek mythology, Achilles is said to have used yarrow for healing and valor.)
- Yarrow can heal spiritual pain and cleanse your aura. If you feel that you've picked up some bad energy, yarrow will help you give it the boot!

## A Yarrow Spell for Newlyweds

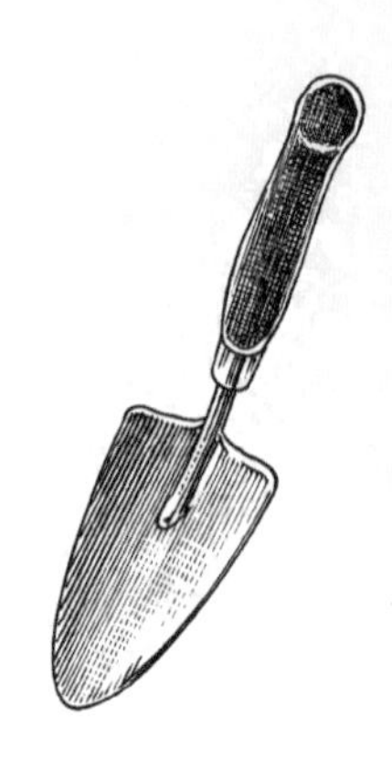

Plant your own yarrow in the garden. As you plant, focus on the intention, which is to enrich the love between you and your significant other. When you harvest the flowers, meditate on what you want your relationship to look like. Picture yourself with your loved one 20, 30, 50 years from now. How does the relationship grow, what does it look like to you?

Allow the flowers to dry for a week. Invite your partner to hang the dried yarrow with you in your bedroom. Share with them the reasons for this little ritual and take the time to say a little prayer of thanks for one another.

# OTHER HERBS AND THEIR MAGICKAL CORRESPONDENCES

If you want to create your own potions and herbal mixes, here is a list of some of the more popular herbs used by witches. By simply placing these plants on your altar during a ritual, it can help a spell be more successful or you might prefer to make your own poppets and pouches, to change the energies surrounding you. (See also the Easy Reference Guide in chapter 7 on pages 194–99; it lists many of the herbs here, as well as key fruits, vegetables, and spices, grouped by spellcasting purpose.)

## Angelica (*Angelica*)

Excellent for protection rituals • Connects with your angel or spirit guide • Used in blessings and cleansings • Guards against hexes • Use with a gold candle to summon the Archangel Michael

## Bay Leaf (*Laurus nobilis*)

Offers all-around protection • Invokes money • Good for business • Improves psychic abilities • Promotes strength and stamina

## Borage (*Borago officinalis*)

Brings about peace and harmony • Promotes courage and strength • Increases psychic abilities • Expands businesses or improves one's chances in work-related matters

## Chervil (*Anthriscus cerefolium*)

Provides protection • Reduces unwanted feelings • Brings a gossip under control • Removes ill-wishing

## Chicory (*Cichorium intybus*)

For frugality • Removes obstacles • Purifies sacred places • Used in healing spells • Aids in weight loss

## **Chives** (*Allium schoenoprasum*)

Offers protection • Drives out negativity • Used in weight-loss spells • Banishes nightmares • Promotes general good health

## **Clover** (*Trifolium*)

Breaks hexes and removes negative spirits • Attracts wealth and money • Promotes good luck, happiness, and harmony

## **Comfrey** (*Symphytum*)

Calms emotions • Promotes safe travel • Heals painful emotions • Cultivates beauty • Attracts wealth and money

## **Coriander or Cilantro** (*Coriandrum sativum*)

For healing spells • Enhances love and relationships • Seeds used for attracting new love • Promotes fertility

## **Dill** (*Anethum graveolens*)

Brings good luck and good fortune • Protects babies • Boosts the sex drive • Promotes success in court cases • Improves well-being • Draws blessings to you • Improves concentration

## **Echinacea** (*Echinacea*)

Used in general health spells ◆ Boosts strength and stamina ◆ For healthy babies ◆ To strengthen relationships

## **Fennel** (*Foeniculum vulgare*)

For healing spells ◆ For cleansing and blessings ◆ Purifies the altar ◆ Brings strength to hopeless situations

## **Fenugreek** (*Trigonella foenum-graecum*)

Boosts finances ◆ Increases luck and prosperity ◆ Promotes success in business ◆ Used in weight-loss spells

## **Feverfew** (*Tanacetum parthenium*)

Improves your mental state ◆ Brings about happiness and joy ◆ Used in rituals for well-being and removing pain

## **Hyssop** (*Hyssopus officinalis*)

Promotes meditation ◆ Used for cleansing and purification ◆ Boosts creativity ◆ Breaks curses and hexes ◆ Sanctifies altars (infuse the herb with water and sprinkle it over magickal areas)

## Lemongrass (*Cymbopogon*)

Wards off evil • Removes hexes • Used in love magick to attract romance • Settles disruptive relationships • Calms fractious children • Used in general healing rituals

## Lemon Verbena (*Aloysia citrodora*)

Helps you break bad habits • Boosts willpower • Calms and purifies • Used in beauty treatments

## Lovage (*Levisticum officinale*)

For love spells • Increases passion in a relationship • Brings happiness and love into families • Used in trinkets and gifts to give to loved ones • Seals friendships

## Milk Thistle (*Silybum marianum*)

Protects you from anything evil • Increases passion • Summons the spirit world • Guards against illness

## Mint (*Mentha*)

Used in healing spells • For safe travel • Invites guides and angels • Promotes money and cash flow • Brings about better luck

## **Nettle** (*Urtica*)

Burn nettle to cleanse altar tools ◆ Protects from dangerous people or places ◆ Casts out evil spirits and ghosts ◆ Hang bundles in your car for protection ◆ Attracts fairies

## **Oregano** (*Origanum vulgare*)

Brings happiness and protection ◆ Promotes good fortune and prosperity ◆ Used in rituals to get over complicated relationships ◆ Protects the home

## **Parsley** (*Petroselinum crispum*)

Used as a charm for luck in competitions ◆ Brings about strength and courage ◆ Twin with turquoise to aid healing ◆ For weddings and other ceremonies ◆ To win a new job ◆ Casts out bad luck and ushers in positivity

## **Sorrel** (*Rumex acetosa*)

To enchant ◆ Entices fairies and elves to the garden ◆ Increases luck and good fortune

## **St. John's Wort** (*Hypericum perforatum*)

Wards off pain and fever ◆ Banishes or removes hexes ◆ Used in protection spells ◆ Prevents nightmares ◆ Lifts a dark mood

Chapter 7

# Foods, Herbs, and Pantry Staples for Health, Home, and Magick

DURING OUR TIME HERE ON EARTH, OUR HUMAN BODY is our only mode of transport; if we want to thrive and live to a grand old age, we must look after it. To simplify things, look at the body as being like an automobile: we wouldn't put the wrong gasoline in our car engine, but we often eat foods that make us feel bloated and unwell. Just as we have to service our car every now and then, we have to do the same with our body and visit our health-care providers for checkups. At the point when our car conks out, we trade it in for another one—a metaphor for the reincarnation process.

The food you eat throughout your life is your fuel, so you need to make sure that, as much as you can, you eat properly. This is a lot easier said than done, especially when we are tempted by the hundreds of wonderful delicacies the twenty-first century has to offer. In the old days, you would visit your local greengrocer, who would sell you seasonal fruits and vegetables, or your granddad might have his own garden and share his homegrown veggies with the family; nowadays, superstores have shelves stocked to the brim with goodies from all over the world, so our choices are vast. Successfully changing your lifestyle requires altering your mind-set: whenever possible, always try to eat organic produce and when you are using any foods for magickal purposes, do the same.

## LEMONS

If there is one fruit you should try to incorporate into your diet every day, it's a lemon! These versatile beauties are jam-packed with so many wonderful health benefits; not only can they be used to cleanse and detox the body, but they can make your hair and your work surfaces shine, too.

When you cut a lemon in half horizontally, you will see that it resembles a sunburst, so it is no wonder witches use them in sun-worshipping rituals. Lemons are usually placed on the altar to represent cosmic energy and the solar deities, and can be a very powerful accessory to your spellcasting.

# Magickal Lemon Water

For a daily detox, drink a large glass of lemon water (hot or cold) mixed with a little honey (preferably sourced locally) every morning. To charge your lemons first, and to give thanks to the sun, follow the ritual below.

## MATERIALS

1 organic lemon, washed and sliced in half

A knife

1 cup (237 ml) of spring water

A saucepan

1–2 teaspoons of honey (preferably local)

## RITUAL

Begin by giving thanks to the sun by venturing outside to see it rise in the morning. As the sun comes into view, hold a half a lemon in each hand, lift your arms above your head for a few minutes, and say:

*"Magnificent sun, I ask of you, bless this fruit, to restore and renew."*

Then take the lemon halves inside and prepare some lemon water to drink.

Begin by cutting the lemon halves into round slices. Place the water and slices in a saucepan and bring it to a boil. Stir in the honey, and after a few minutes strain the liquid into a cup. You can keep this in the fridge for up to three days so whenever you feel like you need to be invigorated, take a few sips and enjoy!

## Clean and Magickally Cleanse with Lemon Power

The walls of houses are renowned for absorbing emotions, so if someone in the home has been ill or others have been quarreling, the house can take on a negative feel. One way you can keep the energies sweet is to use lemons in your daily cleaning routine. Their magickal properties will dissolve bad vibrations almost instantly and leave the home sterile. Most witches are environmentalists and love to make their own cleaning products. It's cheaper on your purse strings, and you'll also be doing your bit to help the planet. Below and on pages 142–43 are some simple recipes for various lemon cleansers for different parts of your house, as well as a recipe for an all-purpose magickal lemon cleanser. Boost the magick good vibes by charging your lemons first using the blessing on the opposite page.

**MAGICK YOUR MICROWAVE CLEAN:** Using a hand juicer, squeeze two halves of a lemon into a glass bowl and place the rind on top. Pour in 1 cup (237 ml) of water and microwave on full power for three to five minutes. Leave the bowl inside the microwave for a further five minutes, then open the door, remove the bowl, and wipe down the inside of the microwave with a clean, damp cloth.

**DESCALING THE KETTLE:** Squeeze the juice of one lemon into the empty kettle and add 2 cups (470 ml) of water. Boil the kettle and let it sit until the water is cool. Your kettle should be left spick-and-span.

**WINDOW AND GLASS CLEANER:** Place three tablespoons of lemon juice in a spray bottle, add 2 cups (470 ml) of water, and then shake well. Spray windows or mirrors and buff up with a clean, dry cloth or some paper towels.

**CLEANING THE TOILET:** Cut a lemon in half and rub some coarse salt into the flesh of the fruit. Rub the lemon around the toilet bowl, getting right under the rim. Flush the toilet, and you'll be pleased to see the gleaming results.

**SPELL AWAY SOAP SCUM:** Due to the acidity found in lemons, soap scum has no chance with this powerful little citrus. Pour pure lemon juice into a spray bottle, squirt your tub or sinks, and simply wipe away with a clean damp cloth.

**SPARKLING TAPS:** You can make your chrome or stainless steel taps and faucets shine like new again by cutting a lemon in half and rubbing the fleshy part all over. Dry off with a clean microfiber cloth.

## Lemon Magick All-Purpose Cleaner

It's time to ditch those convenient bottles of disinfectant sprays and opt for a more organic, witchy way of cleaning. Lemon is a natural sanitizer and will sterilize all surfaces, leaving them smelling fresh, too! (*Note:* This cleaner does not work well with granite, marble, or other natural stone surfaces, or brass.)

### MATERIALS

- 4 organic lemons
- A small paring knife
- A standard glass mason jar with a lid

White vinegar (enough to cover the lemons)

A glass or plastic spray bottle

A strainer

Spring water, as needed

**RITUAL**

Wash the lemons, and then peel the rinds. (Use the lemon juice inside for one of the other recipes in this section or to make lemonade.)

Take the rinds and stuff them into the mason jar until it is filled. Pack them in nice and tight, leaving a large piece of peel at the top so that it prevents the smaller pieces from rising.

Fill the jar with white vinegar, making sure that all the peels are covered, and screw on the lid. Place the jar in a cool, dark place for about a week, checking daily that the peels are still covered.

After a week, strain the liquid into a spray bottle and top up with spring water. Shake well and say this chant:

*"Spick-and-span my home shall be,*
*Bless this concoction, so mote it be."*

You can use this daily to magickally clean your house.

## Lemon Magick

Lemons can be incorporated into lots of spells, as they have so many magickal attributes. On the following pages we suggest are a few examples you can try.

## Lemon Joy to Combat the Blues

We can all get a little down at times; it's really no fun. By performing this ritual, you can reset your mojo and start to feel more positive in the coming days.

**MATERIALS**

- 1 small obsidian stone
- A bowl filled with regular salt
- 1 drawstring pouch
- A few strands of saffron
- Zest of 1 organic lemon
- A yellow candle

**RITUAL**

Before you begin, it is important to cleanse the obsidian, so place in it a bowl of salt for a few hours. This will remove any negative energies the stone may have absorbed.

Take the drawstring pouch and place the saffron, obsidian, and lemon zest inside. Light the yellow candle next to the pouch and say the following incantation three times:

*"Decline and depression fall away, replaced with joy and happier days,*
*My mood is lifted, my mind is clear. All negative thoughts will disappear."*

After you have recited the spell three times, close with the words "*So mote it be.*" Let the candle burn down (do not leave it unattended).

For the next few weeks, make sure you are never far away from your magickal pouch. Place it beside your bed at night and put it in your bag when you venture out to school or work. If you want to cast the spell for someone else, just write down the person's name on a piece of paper and place it inside the pouch, along with the other ingredients. Give the pouch to the person and tell them they must keep it close by at all times.

# Cleanse with Lemon and Sage

If you want to cleanse and bless your home, a witchy way to do this is to use a white sage smudging stick.

For instructions on general smudging of your home, follow the instructions in the ritual on pages 122–23, "A Sage Spell to Rid a Home of Ghosts." Make sure you smudge every room and cubbyhole.

Once your home is completely smudged, take a plastic spray bottle of pure lemon juice and, using a fine spray, squirt all four corners of each room. Your home will now be completely sanitized, blessed, and cleansed of negative energies. Spiders are not the greatest fans of lemons, either, so this type of cleansing also deters the little darlings.

## Dealing with Cranky Individuals

If someone in your family is constantly grumpy or suffers from irritability, they could be feeling this way because they are surrounded by negative energies. Lemons are amazing at drawing out those harmful feelings, leaving a person invigorated and more optimistic.

### MATERIALS

3 organic lemons

A serrated knife

A small dish

½ cup (120 ml) sugar

A medium-size bowl

### RITUAL

Lemons not only work beautifully with the sun but they are also close associates of the moon. The night before you want to cast your spell, chop your lemons into small pieces with the serrated knife (leaving the rind on) and place them on the small dish. Take the dish of lemons outside and leave it overnight on the porch or doorstep under the moon's rays; during the moon's waxing phase is ideal. (If you are in an apartment, you can leave them on a moonlit windowsill.)

The next evening, sprinkle the sugar into the bottom of a medium-size bowl and then place the chopped-up lemons on top. Take the bowl to the person's bedroom and place it either on a nightstand or on a table nearby, or, better still, under their bed. During the nights that follow, the lemons will draw out any negativity, leaving behind a happy mood.

## Protection from Bullying Bosses

We all know that witches shouldn't influence the minds of others when weaving magick, but if your aim is to improve someone's state of mind or leave them feeling happier and more content, then it is absolutely fine. Most bosses are lovely, but it has to be said that there are a fair few who can make their employees' lives miserable. If you love your job but dislike your boss, here is a spell to chase away their demons, leaving them as sweet as can be.

### MATERIALS

- 2 organic lemons
- A serrated knife
- A standard glass mason jar with a lid
- Handful of juniper berries
- 1 tablespoon sugar
- A small piece of paper and a pen
- Spring water, as needed
- 1 white tealight candle

### RITUAL

Leave the lemons outside for two days and two nights to soak up the sunshine and the moon's powerful rays. (If you are in an apartment, you can leave them on a windowsill that receives the rays of both the sun and the moon; a new moon is best.)

Bring the lemons inside and cut them into rounds. Take the mason jar and place the sliced lemons inside, along with a handful of juniper berries and the sugar. Write your boss's name on the piece of paper and place it inside the jar. Fill the vessel with spring water so that it covers the lemons. Light the candle next to the jar. Say this chant three times:

*"No more shall you torment me;*
*Your words are kind and sweet as can be.*
*Your sour mood we all know well*
*Will change now with this lemon spell."*

When you have said the chant three times, close the spell by saying the words "So mote it be." Once the candle has burned down (do not leave it unattended), screw the lid on tightly and shake the jar. Before you head out to work each day, shake the jar again and then unscrew the lid and leave it off until you return.

## CUCUMBERS

The cucumber is probably one of the most useful and nutritious foods to have in the witch's pantry. They are packed with many nutrients—such as vitamins K and B, minerals like potassium and magnesium, and antioxidants—and have a large array of health benefits. Just a few: cucumbers promote hydration, keep your gut healthy, help to lower cholesterol, and ongoing studies show that it might even help control blood sugar. It's a great idea to incorporate cucumber into your diet every day, even if you put a few slices in a sandwich or put some wedges in a small bowl to nibble throughout the day. A recipe for cucumber water is on the opposite page. If you want to keep your skin looking amazing, you might try making your own beauty products, too. They are quick and easy and so much cheaper than the ones you buy in stores.

# Cosmic Cucumber Water

There are so many different recipes for this drink, but after trying many, we think this one is the best.

**Makes 4 glasses**

**Ingredients**

2 whole organic cucumbers, washed

4 cups (1 L) spring water

2 limes

**RITUAL**

Cut the ends off one cucumber, thinly slice about six rounds, and set them to one side.

Peel the other cucumber and then chop the flesh into small pieces.

Place the chopped-up cucumber and spring water into a blender, and blend for three to five minutes. It should be smooth with no lumps. Using a sieve, pour the mixture into a glass jug to strain it. You will be left with a pulp that resembles applesauce. (Reserve the pulp to make a cucumber face mask; see pages 150–51.)

Squeeze the juice of two limes into the cucumber water and stir. Finally, add the cucumber slices for decoration.

You can store the jug of water in the fridge for two–three days. Try to drink a glass every day and before you consume it, say this short mantra three times to empower the cucumber water:

*"This magickal water is blessed with all that is pure."*

# Magick with a Mask

A cucumber face mask is loaded with antioxidants and vitamins; it's wonderful at hydrating the skin, which is especially helpful in the summer, when our skin can dry out. It also acts as a cooling agent and has tightening, anti-aging, and wrinkle-reducing properties, and is known to reduce puffiness and lessen dark circles under the eyes.

This lovely "inside and out" ritual will energize and cleanse your body and leave you feeling happy and relaxed.

**MATERIALS**

A glass of cucumber water and the reserved pulp from the Cosmic Cucumber Water recipe (see page 149)

2 tablespoons aloe vera gel

A small jar

A clean makeup brush

A lavender-scented candle

2–4 cucumber rounds, thinly sliced

**RITUAL**

Drink the cucumber water, and then take the reserved cucumber pulp and mix it with 2 tablespoons of aloe vera gel in the jar.

With a clean makeup brush, apply the cucumber-aloe mixture to your face. Light a lavender-scented candle on your bedroom nightstand or nearby, play some relaxing music if you wish, and lie on the bed. Rest a few slices of cucumber over your eyes.

During this quiet time, relax by concentrating on every part of your body. Release your tongue from the roof of your mouth, making sure your shoulders are not tensed in any way. Let go of all the strain and tension. Imagine that all impurities are leaving your body and visualize yourself in a pale green light. Next, turn your attention to your face and envision the cucumber's properties working their magick and burrowing into every pore of your skin. Say this chant aloud:

*"Beauty is blessed from outside and in,*
*Healing my body and cleansing my skin.*
*So mote it be."*

Then rest on the bed for about 20 minutes. When you arise, blow out the candle and wash your face in clean water and dab dry. Your skin will feel renewed and revitalized, and your mood will be calm and tranquil.

## Organic Cucumber-Rose Water Protective Toner

This toner will help to remove any dark circles and reduce any puffiness around the eyes. It's also good for tightening the pores and smoothing wrinkles, so it's a must-have product to use in your daily beauty regimen. Rose water contains many antioxidants and maintains the pH balance of your skin. One great benefit is that it reduces red facial blotches. From a magickal perspective, rose water is believed to enhance female intuition and can also act as a protection potion, so with this toner you are not only giving your skin the best possible treatment, but you are also safeguarding yourself at the same time.

## MATERIALS

½ organic cucumber

A blender

3 tablespoons spring water, plus ½ cup (120 ml)

A coffee filter, a piece of clean muslin, or a strainer

2 small glass bowls

A small pot

1 tablespoon dried rose petals

A small funnel

A small plastic pump dispenser

## RITUAL

Chop the cucumber (including the skin) into small pieces and place it in the blender. Add 3 tablespoons of spring water. Whip up the mixture for about a minute or two and then strain the liquid with the filter, muslin, or strainer into one of the small glass bowls. When you have done this, the fluid should be bright green and completely lump free. Set aside.

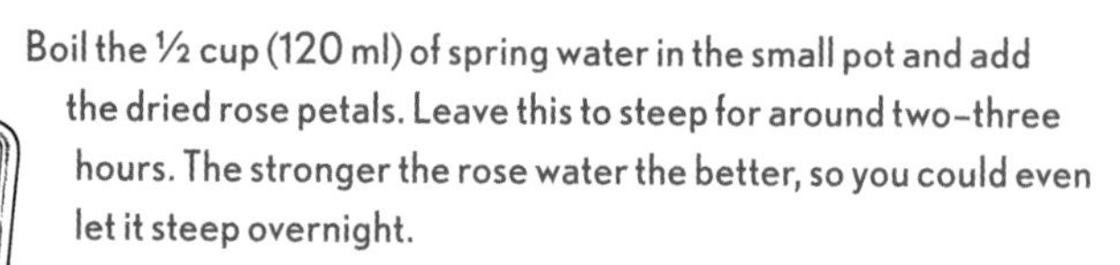

Boil the ½ cup (120 ml) of spring water in the small pot and add the dried rose petals. Leave this to steep for around two–three hours. The stronger the rose water the better, so you could even let it steep overnight.

Once the rosewater liquid is completely cool, strain it into the second glass bowl, making sure there are no petals left. Using the funnel, decant the rose water into the plastic pump dispenser until it is halfway filled. Then use the funnel to decant the cucumber water into the pump dispenser, until the liquid reaches the top of the dispenser. Cover the dispenser and shake it well.

Apply the toner to a cotton ball or pad and dab all over the face. Say this chant aloud:

*"Resplendent skin, outside and in,*
*The magick will now begin."*

Keep the bottle in the fridge or another cool place; it will last up to three days.

# Magickal Cucumber Beauty and Health Tips

**Before you use a cucumber for magickal purposes, always make sure you cleanse and bless it beforehand. Take the cucumber and wash it in bottled spring water, and then dry it with a clean dish towel. Holding it in both hands, say this blessing spell aloud: "From the earth it came and flourished well. This fruit is infused with a powerful spell." Here are ways to incorporate cucumbers into your health and beauty routine:**

- **To soothe eyebrows after plucking or waxing**, finely slice two pieces of cucumber and place them on your brows to reduce any redness or swelling.
- **To treat dandruff:** Peel a whole cucumber and grate it into a bowl. Add 1 tablespoon of salt and whisk in an egg. Mix together well and then massage the mixture into your hair and leave for one hour. Rinse with clean water.
- **For dried, cracked lips,** slice a thin piece of cucumber lengthwise and sprinkle it lightly with sugar. Place it on the lips for five minutes.
- **To treat mild sunburn,** peel a whole cucumber and chop it into small pieces. Transfer it to a blender and add 1 tablespoon of aloe vera gel and ½ cup (120 ml) of water. Whip up the m ixture until it resembles a clear green liquid. Strain into a plastic spray bottle. Spray it over the skin and rub it into the affected area with your hands.

- **To ease hangover headaches,** eat a few slices of cucumber before you go to bed.
- **To eliminate bad breath,** take a slice of a cucumber and place it on the roof of your mouth. The properties in cucumber help kill bad bacteria.

# Stress-Busting Spell

Many people believe that just the smell of a cucumber can alleviate stress and tension, so if you're worried about something or someone is driving you mad, try this spell.

## MATERIALS

1 organic cucumber

A knife

A saucepan

Spring water, as needed

A purple candle

A strainer

A mug

## RITUAL

Take the cucumber and slice it thinly. Place the pieces in the saucepan and pour in enough spring water to cover the pieces. Bring to a boil.

Light a purple candle near the stove, but at a safe distance, and let it burn while the tonic is boiling. After a few minutes, keeping the candle lit (but not unattended), turn off the stove and let the mixture cool. Once cooled, strain the liquid into the mug. Say this chant aloud seven times:

> ***"This tonic is charmed, I am now armed.***
> ***Composed and strong, my stress is gone."***

When you have completed the spell, close by saying the words "So mote it be." Drink the entire contents of the cup, and then blow out the candle. Your mood will now be calm and composed.

# Fertility Spell

This fertility spell is performed in two phases. For the first phase, on a full moon, scrape the seeds out of a cucumber and dry them on a paper towel for a few days or until they no longer contain any moisture. Once the seeds are dried, on the first night of the next new moon, perform the second phase as follows.

## MATERIALS

- A pentagram (can be an image of one or a physical one)
- 2 small red candles
- 1 large white altar candle
- The dried cucumber seeds in a small bowl
- (See note below for additional materials if you're performing the spell for someone else)

## RITUAL

Place the pentagram in the center of your altar. Put the red candles on either side of the pentagram and the white candle at the back in the center. Position the cucumber seeds at the front.

****NOTE***: If you're casting the spell on behalf of someone else, it's crucial to have a photograph of them or a lock of their hair placed on top of the pentagram on the altar.

Light the candles and stare at the flames for about five minutes and envision yourself (or a specific person who wants to become pregnant) cradling a child. Say this incantation thirteen times with intention:

*"New moon shines bright, this magickal night,*
*Hear my plight and aid me now.*
*This empty womb will be full soon, of cheerful child,*
*Sweet and mild."*

When you have said the spell, close it by saying, "So mote it be." Leave everything in situ on the altar until the candles have burned down (do not leave it unattended). You (or the person you did the spell for) should eat a few of the cucumber seeds before making love.

## Protection Spell When You're Out and About

Take one pair of shoes for each person in the house (ones worn regularly) and line them all up on a worktable. Light a white tealight candle behind each pair of shoes. Take a cucumber and cut it in half. Rub the fleshy part of the cucumber onto the soles of each shoe. While you are doing this, recite the following chant over and over again until you have finished:

*"When you are out and away from home,*
*I will guard you while you roam."*

When you have finished anointing all the shoes, close the spell by saying, "So mote it be." When you and your loved ones are out and about, the magick of the spell will help protect all of you from danger.

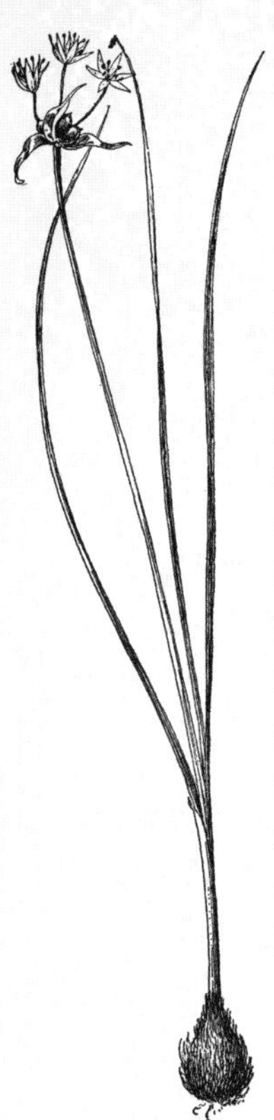

## GARLIC

This is one food staple that really should be in the larder at all times. For witches with a green thumb, garlic is easy to grow, either in garden soil or by planting wild garlic in borders. In the fall, plant a bulb with the pointed part facing upward and harvest around June and July. It not only tastes great and is an excellent accompaniment to your recipes, but it is immersed in legend. Garlic has been incorporated in healing and magick since ancient times. Our ancestors would use it to ward off illness and it was even considered a deterrent in times of plague. One tradition was to rub garlic into the horns of cattle to keep them safe and well. Some witches like to make an offering of garlic to the Greek goddess Hecate—as she was said to favor it—by leaving a garlic clove at a crossroads to honor her. It's not uncommon to see a string of garlic bulbs hanging in a witch's kitchen.

Garlic is rich in antioxidants, vitamins, and minerals. It has antimicrobial properties that can help your body fight many types of infection; antioxidant components in garlic are believed to slow down the aging process; and, for arthritis sufferers, garlic's allicin and thiacremonone sulfur compounds work as anti-inflammatories that reduce pain and stiffness.

If you (and your partner!) don't mind the smell or taste of garlic, drinking garlic water can help you take advantage of this bulb's healthful qualities. Boil 1 cup (237 ml) of water and set it aside until it is lukewarm.

Add three peeled garlic cloves and let them steep for 20 minutes. Remove the garlic pieces and drink the water. (*Note*: Do not ingest large amounts of garlic if you have a bleeding disorder or are taking blood-clotting medication, if you have diabetes, if you have IBS or acid reflux, if you are breastfeeding, or for at least two weeks before a planned surgery.)

## Harmonious Plant Pesticide

Remember, even the peskiest of bugs have as much right as we do to live out a safe and carefree life. Of course, knowing that doesn't help when we lovingly grow our broccoli and cabbage, only to find them decimated once they start to get bigger. If you want to stop bugs from eating your prized crops or killing off your flowers, don't reach for store-bought pesticides. These can be toxic and harmful to the environment, and if you are growing produce to eat, it's not a very healthy way to go. Instead, why not try the witchy way and make some of your very own garlic insecticides?

Boil 1 cup (237 ml) of water and turn off the heat. Add three or four cloves of crushed garlic and let them steep in the water for 30 minutes. Strain the garlic with a sieve until you are left with just the liquid. Gaze into the mixture and say this chant seven times:

***"Bugs, please be on your way, choose another plant, if you may."***

When cooled, fill a spray bottle halfway with spring water and top it up with the garlic water you've just made. To finish, add a tiny drop of liquid soap and swirl it around. Once or twice a week, shake well and spray this mixture directly onto the plants and around the area where you want to keep the pests out. It's always nice to plant a little variety of veggies just for the insects and leave it free of any pesticides, which helps keep the natural harmony in balance.

## Natural Mosquito Repellent

A natural way to keep mosquitoes at bay is to make a garlic spray. Many a dream holiday has been ruined by mosquito bites. They are painful and itchy—and, depending where in the world you are, they can cause disease. Take three bulbs of garlic (skins and all) and with the side of a cleaver or a large knife, press down on the cloves to release the juices. Transfer the garlic into 3 cups (710 ml) of boiling water and simmer for 30 minutes. Remove the liquid from the heat and use a potato masher to compress the garlic and release more of its goodness. Place the mixture back on the heat for another five minutes and then strain the water into a glass jug. Let it cool. Pour the liquid into a plastic spray bottle and then add ten drops of lavender oil or tea tree oil. This not only helps to mask the smell of the garlic, but mosquitos don't like these two scented oils, either. Shake well. Spray this on your clothes or body. (*Note:* Before putting this on your skin, patch-test a small area of skin first for 24 hours.) You'll be amazed at how well it works!

## Garlic Anointing Oil

Not only is garlic oil wonderful for cooking, but it is also great for anointing candles when you are casting any kind of banishing spells. It's terrific for some beauty treatments, too! Garlic oil is a must-have for all witches and very simple to make. Take a whole bulb of garlic and separate the pieces by pressing them apart with the flat side of a large knife. Peel the garlic cloves and then cut them in half lengthwise. Heat 4 tablespoons of olive oil in a pan and add the garlic. Cook gently until it browns. Remove the garlic and let the oil cool. Transfer the oil into a small glass bottle, and then chop the cooked garlic into small pieces and drop them into the bottle, too. Before you secure the lid, say this mantra three times:

***"Charged with blessings, bestowed with power,***
***Steeped in magick, hour after hour."***

Store the bottle in a cool place. This only has a three- to four-week shelf life, so you will need to use it quickly.

# More Magickal Garlic Tips

**This vegetable is all-powerful, even before any magick takes place, but it's always a nice idea to charge it before use. Hold it in your hand and say this chant: "*I see your power, I charge you times three, be bold in your magick, so mote it be.*"**

**Here are some additional ways you can use garlic in your healing, beauty, and home rituals:**

- To ease congestion, chop up some garlic cloves and place them in a small jar. Cover the garlic cloves with honey and set aside for twenty-four hours. Take 1 teaspoon of the mixture every few hours or until your congestion subsides (see note on page 160 about precautions).
- To keep nails healthy, rub a tiny amount of garlic oil on yellowing nails morning and night for a few weeks. They should lose the yellow tinge.
- For a natural disinfectant to use around the house, chop three to four cloves of garlic and place them inside a plastic spray bottle. Fill to the top with 2 cups (470 ml) of water. Add any type of citrus essential oil to make it smell sweet.
- Protect yourself from the evil eye by keeping a piece of garlic in your pocket throughout the day.
- Wipe the blade of your athame with a clove of peeled garlic to enhance its magick.

# Protect Your Home from Evil Spirits

If you believe your house is haunted or you simply want to protect it from malevolent spirits, this spell will ward off any evil and leave the energies in your home squeaky clean.

## MATERIALS

7 white tealight candles

1 bulb garlic (whole)

1 garlic clove, peeled

## RITUAL

Place the candles in a circle on your altar and light them. Rest the garlic bulb and the garlic clove in the center. Say this chant thirteen times:

*"I place a shield around this home,*
*No evil spirits here shall roam."*

When you have said the spell, close the ritual by saying the words "So mote it be."

When the candles have burned down (do not leave them unattended), take the single clove of garlic and rub it all around the doorframes of each entry point in the house. Next, you must hang the whole bulb of garlic somewhere near the front door. You could try attaching some yarn or string to the tip of the bulb to fasten. Perform this spell twice a year to ensure that your house remains free from spirits.

(***NOTE:*** Using the exact same method above, you can also deter thieves from breaking into your house. Just change the chant wording to: "No evil feet will cross my path, I cast you out with all my wrath.")

## Reverse a Curse

If you know you have been cursed, or even if you just suspect it, you need to act fast. Curses can cause no end of trouble and bring a string of bad luck to you and even to those close to you.

### MATERIALS

- A small mirror
- 1 clove garlic
- A white spell candle and candleholder

### RITUAL

Find a small mirror—it can be a hand mirror or a compact—but make sure it's not one you will want to use again. With a mortar and pestle, mash a clove of garlic into a pulp and smear it around the frame of the mirror. Lay the mirror on a flat surface with the reflective side faceup. Put the candle in its holder, position it on the top of the mirror, and then light it. Say this chant seven times:

*"Evil eyes I reflect, my body,*
*My family I protect,*
*Return the curse from where it came,*
*Never to visit here again."*

When you have finished reciting the spell, close the ritual by adding the words "So mote it be."

Drip a little bit of wax from the candle onto the mirror and then let the candle burn down (do not leave it unattended). Place the mirror facing outward in a window of your home and the curse will be broken.

# To Dispel Unwanted Attention

Using garlic in rituals to get rid of unwelcome attention has been a practice for centuries. If you have a clingy ex, or even if you have an unwanted admirer, this spell will distract that individual, leaving you free to live your life in peace.

## MATERIALS

- Several cloves of garlic
- A small fireproof dish
- A long-handled lighter
- A pen and a small piece of paper
- A locket necklace or an empty matchbox

## RITUAL

On a waning moon, remove the papery skin from the garlic cloves and place them in a fireproof dish. It's best to do this in the kitchen sink because of the fire risk. With a long-handled lighter, set fire to the skins until all that remains are the ashes. This can take a few minutes because they don't burn quickly.

Next, write the name of the person you want to cast away on the piece of paper, followed by the words With all good intentions. Burn this in the dish as well. When the ashes are cool, mix them together and transfer as much of the ash as possible into the locket. Wear the necklace for a few weeks, especially when you might be around the person who is bothering you. For those who don't wear jewelry, you can empty the ashes into a matchbox. It's important to keep these ashes on your person, so carry the box in your pocket.

# ONIONS

Most people add onions to their weekly shopping lists, since they have so many culinary uses. But onions also contain a wealth of antioxidants that are extremely efficient at counterbalancing free radicals in the body; they are high in vitamin C and can help boost your immune system. They are excellent for heart health and thin the blood. (*Note:* If you are taking blood thinners, have a blood-clotting disorder or condition, or are scheduled for surgery, you should avoid onions or speak to your health-care practitioner before using or consuming them.) Onions even work wonderfully as a natural insect repellent.

The humble onion has been steeped in lore for millennia. Ancient Egyptians buried their pharaohs with onions to keep away evil spirits, and the Romans believed onions cured everything from toothaches to insomnia (having a few slices of raw onion in a sandwich or salad every day is actually said to help promote sleep). In English folklore, onions were sliced in half and placed in the home to "absorb" germs.

Because onions have been associated with magick for so long, it is not surprising that many spells call for them. Probably the most common spells are those used in love magick—typically to rekindle a relationship or bring back a lost love. It can be heartbreaking when a partner leaves, especially if you don't want the relationship to end, but everything does happen in life for a reason. Shawn and I tend to steer away from

casting spells to bring back lost loves because it's not ethical to magickally influence another person's mind. You would be better to perform a ritual to calm down your emotions and move on.

On the following pages are spells focusing on healing, empowering your relationship, and easing various stressors. (*Note*: Do not ingest large amounts of onion if you have a bleeding disorder or are taking blood-clotting medication, if you have diabetes, if you have IBS or acid reflux, or for at least two weeks before a planned surgery.)

## Two Elixirs for Easing Colds

These ancient remedies will help soothe a cough or sore throat if you or someone in your family is suffering from a cold.

### Recipe 1: Onion Syrup

**Makes 1 medium-size jar**

**Ingredients**

1 onion, skin removed

6–12 tablespoons sugar

Slice the onion into rounds. Place one layer of onion inside a medium-size jar (with a screw-top lid). (Make sure the onion slices fit inside the jar; you may need to cut the onion up a little, depending on its size.) Then cover the layer of onion with 1 tablespoon of sugar. Repeat this process until you have run out of onion.

Screw the lid on the jar and let it steep for six hours. Say this chant aloud:

*"This tincture will ease,*
*A cold it will cure,*
*The illness will leave,*
*It shall be no more."*

When you open the jar, it will have formed a tincture. Drain the liquid and give a tablespoon to the sufferer. Store the mixture in the refrigerator for two to three days.

## Recipe 2: Milky Onion Tea

This method is wonderful for soothing a sore throat.

**Makes 1 cup**

**Ingredients**

- 1 onion, skin removed
- 1 cup (237 ml) milk
- 1 tablespoon honey (preferably local)

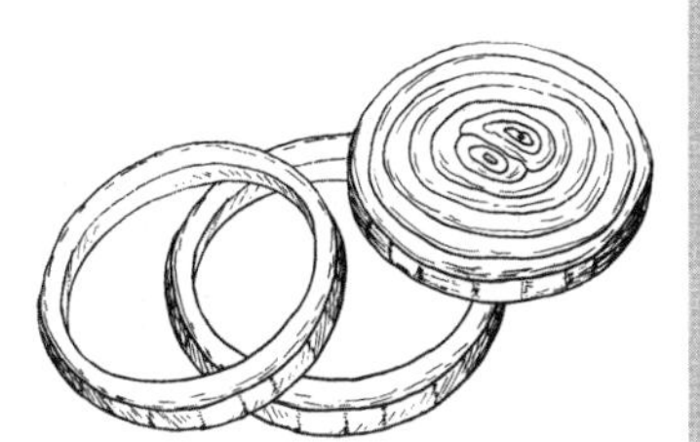

Slice up the onion and place it in a saucepan.

Add the milk and let it simmer for about ten minutes or until the onions are somewhat soft.

While it's hot, strain the liquid into a mug and add the honey.

Let it cool slightly, and sip slowly.

## Bring Longevity to a Relationship

This spell is for those with long-term partners. It will ensure that your relationship has longevity and remains happy and healthy.

**MATERIALS**

1 onion

1 green spell candle

**RITUAL**

On the evening of a waxing moon phase, set up your altar and place the onion on the surface. Position the candle nearby and light it. Say this chant seven times:

*"Buried in earth,*
*These roots will grow,*
*For years to come,*
*Our love will flow."*

When you have said the spell, close the ritual by saying the words "So mote it be."

Let the candle burn down. Dig a large enough hole in the garden to fit the onion and then bury it with the roots pointing downward; cover it up with soil. If you don't have a garden, you can fill a pot with earth and bury it the same way, placing it outside on a patio or by the front door. As the shoots start to emerge in the coming months, your relationship will get stronger.

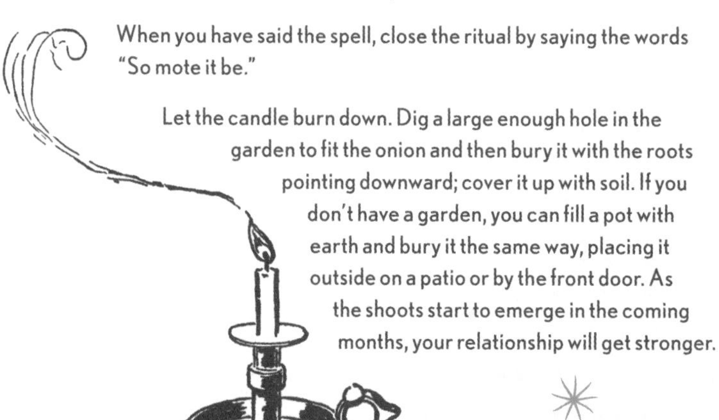

## To Reveal the Truth

If you have your suspicions that someone isn't telling you the truth, it can leave you feeling frustrated and unhappy. This spell will reveal all, but it might take around a month to work.

### MATERIALS

- A pale blue candle
- 1 onion
- A small knife
- 1 long straight pin

### RITUAL

On a new moon phase, light the candle in the kitchen. Slice the top off the onion with the knife. Think of the person you believe is keeping things from you. See them in your mind's eye and visualize them telling you the truth. Push the pin all the way into the top of the onion and say this chant:

*"As I peel, the truth I reveal."*

Peel away the first layer of onion and recite the chant once more. Repeat this until you are left with just a tiny piece of onion and the pin. Save the outer onion pieces and cook a dish using a few of the layers. Serve the food to the one keeping the secret and bury the tiny piece of onion and the pin in some soil. The truth will eventually come out.

## Cast Out Money Worries

There's no worse feeling than not having enough money to manage. This can cause sleeplessness, sadness, hopelessness, and depression. Not only will this spell stop you from fretting over your finances, but it should send a bit of a cash injection your way, too. (*Note*: This spell involves setting fire to onion skin, so it's very important that you do this safely. If you have a wood-burning stove or a firepit, you can burn the onion in there, but for those who don't, you can use a fireproof dish. Make sure to have a large pot of water on hand.)

### MATERIALS

1 onion

A green candle

A yellow candle

A fireproof dish

A lighter

### RITUAL

On the Wednesday of a waning moon, peel the skin from the onion (reserve the skin) and light the candles. Hold the peeled onion in your hands and say this chant:

*"However much I am in debt,*
*No more shall I fuss and fret.*
*A stash of cash will come my way*
*And make for a better, brighter day.*
*So mote it be."*

Toss the onion skin into an open fire or burn the skin in the fireproof dish. Let the candles burn all the way down (make sure not to leave them unattended). Cook a meal with the onion and eat it the very same day.

## More Magickal Onion Tips

**As with all things magickal, you must cleanse and bless the onion before it can be used. Take an unpeeled onion and place it on your third-eye chakra; hold it there for around thirty seconds. Visualize a beam of powerful light radiating from your third eye and being sent to the vegetable. In your mind, tell the onion that you are filling it with healing energy and that it is now ready to work for you as you wish.**

**Here are some additional ways you can use onions in your spellwork:**

- Place a few slices of raw onion under the welcome mat for use in spells to ward off unwanted visitors.
- Hang onions in the home to protect the house from any negative vibes.
- Incorporate onions into any healing spells to help boost their power.
- Place an onion under your pillow to receive psychic dreams about your future partner.

# OLIVE OIL

The amazing health-giving properties of olive oil are widely known. Long a common ingredient in Mediterranean cuisine, many of us are now replacing our usual cooking fats with this liquid gold and incorporating it into our everyday lives. It reduces the risk of heart disease and stroke, lowers blood pressure and cholesterol, and may even help to ward off certain types of cancer. Olive oil has also been used in religious rituals and as an ingredient in beauty formulations for millennia in cultures from Greece and Rome to North Africa and Asia Minor.

## Body Magick with Olive Oil

Adding more olive oil to your diet will do your body good, and including it in your magickal practices will make a real difference in your spells. (*Note:* Applying olive oil directly to the skin is not recommended for those with oily or acne-prone skin.) Boost the magickal power inherent in olive oil by charging it first: pour the oil into a bowl and stare into it, sending your positive intent directly to it. After a few minutes, say these words: "I charge this oil with all things positive. All negative vibes shall be gone."

**OLIVE OIL FOR SKIN:** Many witches don't go for store-bought creams and moisturizers. They tend to be wildly expensive, and the ingredients on the labels may be mystifying. By purchasing a good-quality bottle of olive oil as your moisturizer, you can give your skin everything it needs to look and feel great.

**EYE-MAKEUP REMOVER:** If you want healthy-looking skin, never ever go to bed with your makeup on. It clogs up the pores and can cause premature ageing. Leanna's grandmother told her that for every night you sleep with your makeup on, your face will age a day quicker. Simply add a few drops of olive oil to a cotton pad and wipe away your makeup before you go to bed.

**NIGHT CREAM:** Using a blend of petroleum jelly and olive oil at night can help to reduce dark rings and puffiness under the eyes. In an airtight, clean jar, mix 3 tablespoons of petroleum jelly with 3 tablespoons of olive oil. Make sure the mixture is completed blended. Rub a tiny amount under your eyes before bedtime, and you'll wake up looking adorable.

**OLIVE OIL FOR GLOSSY HAIR:** To encourage hair growth, gently heat ½ cup (120 ml) of olive oil with a clove of peeled, crushed garlic. Don't let it boil; you just want to heat it up. Set it aside and let it cool. Next, with a sieve, strain out the garlic until you are left with just the oil. You can transfer this into a bottle or jar and store it in a cool place. Massage a few tablespoons of the oil onto clean, wet hair and leave for around three to five minutes. Rinse thoroughly.

For dandruff, using the same method above, heat the oil and replace the garlic with a tablespoon of lemon juice. This will leave the hair glossy and dandruff free.

**STOP SNORING:** There's nothing worse than trying to sleep when you have a partner at your side making wild-animal noises. According to some research, the anti-inflammatory properties found in olive oil help to stop this annoying nighttime occurrence. In a small glass place a few tablespoons of olive oil and 1 teaspoon of honey, and mix well. Make sure the snorer has a few sips of this tincture before going to sleep. This also helps to soothe a sore throat, so it is a wonderful home remedy for colds.

# More Magickal Olive Oil Tips

**Here are some additional ways you can use olive oil in your healing, beauty, and home rituals. Make sure to magickally charge the oil first, as discussed on page 174.**

- For achy muscles, mix ½ teaspoon of cayenne pepper with 3 tablespoons of olive oil and massage into the affected area. (*Note*: Do a patch test first for 24 hours to make sure you do not have a reaction to the capsicum in cayenne. Do not use this if you have sensitive skin. Also, keep this mixture away from your eyes.)
- Mix a few drops of your favorite fragrant essential oil with a tablespoon of olive oil and add the mixture to your bubble bath.
- To avoid nicks and cuts when shaving, massage olive oil into your legs or face before using your razor. You'll get a lovely smooth shave.
- To help your feline familiar, add a few drops of olive oil to their food every once in a while. This stops furballs and leaves kitties' coats soft and shiny.

## Magickal Base Oil

Witches use oils every day in their spells and rituals, and olive oil is probably the purest and best of all to use. Infusing a variety of herbs into the oil makes it very effective as an anointing oil, which can be used to bless your candles and give more power to a spell. When infusing oils and herbs, you will need to energize the mixture by steeping the herbs in the oil for at least twenty-four hours. This is best done in a bowl. Next, light a white tealight candle at a safe distance from the oil and say this chant:

***"Plant and oil combine as one, with powerful vibes, the liquid is done."***

Let the candle burn for a few hours (attended) and then blow it out. With a little funnel, transfer the oil into a small bottle. Make sure you add a few herb leaves to the bottle, too, as these will keep the magick in! Store the oil in a cool place for up to three months. After this time, the potency will decrease so you will have to make some more. See chapter 8 for more on making magickal oils.

## A Get-Well Spell

If you or someone you know is unwell—whether physically or spiritually run-down—and a swift pick-me-up is needed, this three-day ritual should improve things. Keep in mind that if you're casting a spell on someone else's behalf, it's always best to ask their permission first.

## MATERIALS

- A yellow candle
- A small bowl of rainwater
- A paper towel or clean cloth
- A knife
- A mortar and pestle
- A small bottle of Magickal Base Oil (see page 177)
- ½ teaspoon dried apple blossom
- Pinch of dried lavender
- A candleholder
- A photograph of the person needing healing

## RITUAL

To begin, cleanse the length of the candle with the rainwater, trickling it over the bowl for a few minutes; then dry it with the paper towel or cloth. With the knife, gently carve two lines horizontally into the candle, evenly spaced, creating three sections. Using a mortar and pestle, mix the oil together with the apple blossom and the lavender. If you can't get hold of apple blossom, you can substitute dried rosemary for it.

### Day 1

Anoint the candle with the Magickal Base Oil by applying a tiny amount of the oil onto your finger and then massaging it into the wax. You don't want the candle to be wet, so use very small amounts of the oil. Place the candle in the holder and put it on your altar. Rest the photograph of the sufferer and the bottle of Magickal Base Oil on the altar and light the candle. Say this chant seven times:

*"As this candle flame burns today, your illness will start to melt away."*

Dip your finger into the bottle of oil and press it onto the face of the person in the photograph. Let the candle burn down (do not leave it unattended) to the first horizontal line you engraved and then blow it out.

### Day 2

Repeat the procedure as for day 1 and let the candle flame burn down to the second line you engraved. Dab the photograph once again with the oil.

### Day 3

Repeat the ritual as you did on days 1 and 2 but, this time, after the chant, close the spell by saying, "And now you are healed, so mote it be." Let the candle burn all the way down.

Give the picture and the bottle of oil to the sufferer and tell them to dab a little oil on their forehead every night (or, if the spell is for you, dab the oil on your own forehead). They (or you) should start to feel better within a few days. *Note*: Never abandon this spell halfway through, as you'll get disappointing results.

## Communicate Your Fears to Your Guide, God, or Goddess

There are times when we have so much to worry about that we can make ourselves ill. You've probably said to yourself in times like these: "If only I could wave a magick wand to make everything better." Olive oil has been used for centuries as a carrier oil to connect with the God and Goddess, and when you make a direct connection with those upstairs, they will always visit and help if they can. Whichever deity you worship, you can make contact with them—or your spirit guide or angel—by performing this ceremony.

### MATERIALS

- Handful of bath salts
- 1 tablespoon olive oil
- 5 drops peppermint essential oil
- 2–3 cream-colored candles

### RITUAL

On the evening of a new moon phase, draw a bath and toss in the bath salts and olive oil. Add the peppermint oil to the water and swirl it around. Place a few cream-colored candles around your bathroom and light them. Turn off any overhead lights and step into the water. Relax back to begin your meditation.

Feeling the warmth of the water all over you, visualize yourself bathed in lavender-colored light. Focus on your breathing, keeping it steady. Continue with this relaxation for about ten minutes. Next, say this chant thirteen times:

*"I call down [my guide–my angel–my God / Goddess,*
*whichever one you worship].*
*Cleanse me in your ethereal light,*
*Communicate with me this night."*

Rest in the tub until you are ready to get out. Once you have dried your body, blow out the candles and go straight to bed, unclothed. Being naked will bring better results, as you will not have any earthly trappings to block the communication. You can continue with your meditation or speak to your spirit guide or higher power telepathically in your mind, relaying to them all your troubles and fears. Ask them for their help. Tell them what you want to happen and ask them to intervene and make your worry disappear.

Your spiritual carer can connect with you in many different ways. You could have a vivid dream that you might need to interpret in the morning, or you might actually feel their presence as you are just drifting off to sleep. They always help if they are allowed to. If you need to learn a particular lesson in life, they might not be able to interfere but, rest assured, they will bring you comfort and lessen your stress. They never ignore your prayers.

## MAGICKAL INGREDIENTS

Many of the foods in your kitchen contain magickal properties that can be used in spellcraft, either as altar items during spellcasting or in culinary recipes boosted by magick. Mealtimes can be more than just occasions to shovel food into your mouth; take the time to start thinking about what you eat and understand the hidden benefits of ingredients and what they might symbolize.

On pages 184–93 are A to Z lists of fruits, vegetables, and spices and their magickal properties. Of course, we haven't listed every single fruit, vegetable, or spice, or this book would turn into an encyclopedia, but we included some of the more common ones that you might start to think differently about. Almost any food staple can be included in a specific ritual, depending on its magickal qualities. And eating foods that are magickally empowered will boost a spell even more. Once you know which foods relate to the spell or situation you are trying to achieve, you can mix and match, and try including them in your daily meals. An Easy Reference Guide is included at the end of the A to Z lists, on pages 194–99.

For example, if you want to cast a spell to enhance your divination and psychic awareness, you would refer to page 195 of the Easy Reference Guide for a list of foods that will help with the matter at hand; some of the foods you might like to incorporate in your spellcasting would be blueberries, cherries, cinnamon, dates, grapefruit, lettuce, mushrooms, and purple grapes. You might want to make a magickal smoothie, including two or three of these foods or you may prefer to perform a candle ritual, placing a few of the foodstuffs on your altar.

Another example would be if you were lacking in confidence and needed to find some inner strength, you would again consult the Easy Reference Guide on page 199 and pick out a few food items that represent strength and courage, like bay leaves, garlic, or spinach. While you are preparing your meal, you could burn a candle and imagine the ingredients giving you courage.

# Grow Your Own

We all know that eating lots of fruits and veggies is super healthy, but they are so much more than that! As we have just discussed, every plant-based food possesses some kind of magickal property that can be incorporated into your spells and rituals.

Of course, the power the plant holds is rocketed to another level if you grow it yourself (see page 103). Taking a simple seed and nurturing it until it blossoms into a strong and vigorous plant will give any spell that extra clout.

Not everyone can grow their own, though, and those without a garden can buy store-bought produce; this is perfectly okay, too. Even if you only have a small area, you can grow herbs and vegetables on a sunny patio or balcony quite successfully. Just fill a pot with soil, sow your seeds, and water them regularly.

## Fruits

From a magickal perspective, fruits are potent and can be used in a variety of ways. If you are performing spells with fruit, always honor them beforehand by casting a blessing. Holding the fruit in your left hand (nearest to the heart), say this short sentence: "I call upon Mother Earth, to bless this food with all that is good and pure, so mote it be."

**APPLE** Helps with broken heart issues, boosts sex and passion, increases overall happiness, stengthens love spells to attract a lover

**APRICOT** Attracts love, maintains a healthy relationship, promotes harmony in families and friendships

**AVOCADO** Soothes tempers; increases sexual appetite, fertility, beauty, and happiness in families; promotes motherhood; facilitates better communication in relationships; helps achieve goals; encourages confidence and self-empowerment; enhances natural beauty; increases sex and passion, and growth in the garden; offers protection for nature and the environment

**BANANA** Promotes creativity, money, happiness, luck in families, connecting to spiritual matters, sexual prowess in men

**BLACKBERRY**

Branches: Offer all-around protection
Berries: For money magick and fertility

**BLUEBERRY** Strengthens communication, confers protection from psychic attack, increases natural beauty, boosts lust and sex, aids in weight loss

**CANTALOUPE** Boosts motivation, spiritual protection, happiness and joy

### CHERRY

Red or yellow cherry: Encourages divination and clairvoyance, enhances prophetic dreams, heals emotional distress, fosters friendships, deters negative relationships, attracts love
Black cherry: Used for banishments and protection

### COCONUT

Coconut meat: Enhances fidelity, and offers protection for a person and protection for a home
Coconut oil: Used in beauty regimens, including hair conditioning

**CRANBERRY** Promotes love and romance, used in cleansing, enhances courage, offers all-around protection, aids in achieving your aspirations

**DATE** Used in love spells to attract a mate or sweeten a relationship, heals friendships after disagreements, boosts physical energy, enhances psychic visions and clairvoyance

**ELDERBERRY** Offers protection from negative emotions, guards against psychic attack, increases wisdom and understanding, strengthens spirit communication, enhances fidelity

**GRAPEFRUIT** Boosts self-confidence, emotional happiness, and female fertility; banishes negative energies; removes hexes and curses; promotes creativity; enhances psychic visions, increases emotional strength

### GRAPE

Green grape: Promotes romance and passion, good luck, wealth and good fortune
Red grape: Enhances fertility, motivation, lust, strength
Purple grape: Used in divination, enhances psychic visions and spirit communication

**KIWI** Valuable in seeking the truth; combats insomnia; encourages joy and happiness, good fortune, sex and passion

**LEMON** Perfect for sun magick rituals, removes hexes and curses, banishes evil, brightens mood, spurs creativity, energizes, part of many friendship blessings, cures bad behavior in pets, used in weight-loss spells, repels the evil eye

**LIME** Heals emotional stress or pain, invokes spiritual protection, vigor and strength, protection from negativity, banishes money troubles, distracts jealous friends or family members

**LYCHEE** Brings happiness into life, boosts energy, increases clairvoyant abilities, motivates, used in love magick rituals to sweeten a partner's mood

**MANDARIN ORANGE** Invites friendships, cultivates youth and beauty, promotes restful sleep, protects the home, encourages happiness and joy, used in sun-magick rituals

**OLIVE** Promotes happiness, boosts sexual prowess in men, confers wisdom, reveals secrets, ushers in peacefulness and tranquility, helps with fertility, offers all-around protection (olive leaf), an all-purpose anointing oil

**ORANGE** Aids creativity and enhances dreams, invokes money, increases opportunities, promotes angelic communication, stops obsessive thinking, used in love magick, helps with fertility, strengthens friendships

**PASSION FRUIT** Heals emotional pain, boosts lust and passion, promotes love and fidelity, heightens dream-sleep, helps in connecting with the astral body

**PEACH** Cultivates happiness, attracts love, increases female fertility, boosts wisdom and knowledge, used in exorcisms, aids in weight loss, provides all-around protection

**PEAR** Encourages sex and passion, invokes money, promotes health and well-being

**PINEAPPLE** Boosts imagination, alleviates stress, clears away tensions, promotes luck and happiness, opens doors to opportunities, moves aside creative blockages

**PLUM** Promotes sleep, lust and sex magick, money and business, love and marriage

**POMEGRANATE** Offers all-around protection, boosts spiritual communication, encourages love and sex, can be used to represent blood or internal organs in a spell

**PRUNE** Promotes beauty, encourages love and passion, counters insomnia or sleep disorders, promotes long life, removes obstacles

**QUINCE** Brings about a settled home life, encourages happiness and contentment, helps to accomplish goals, offers spiritual protection, attracts new lovers, increases fertility

**RAISIN** Boosts wisdom and knowledge, concentration, and longevity; improves sexual performance; aids in weight loss; increases willpower

**RASPBERRY** Promotes fertility, patience, luck, and happiness; invokes strength in marriage matters; encourages love; boosts courage; can be used to represent blood in a spell

**STRAWBERRY** Boosts fertility, helps with weight loss, increases willpower, heals the heart after relationship breakups, reveals cheating partners and infidelity

**TOMATO** Invokes money, prosperity, and good fortune; fosters love and relationships; offers protection from any form of evil thing or person; helps in overcoming bad habits; boosts willpower

**WATERMELON** Boosts sex drive and counters impotence; brings on good fortune, happiness, and joy; releases stress and anxiety, deepens meditation

## Vegetables

As mentioned earlier, there are countless ways we can use veggies in our spellwork, either by including them in magickal recipes or by placing them as offerings on our altar when a spell commences. The list below includes the magickal properties of the most common vegetables.

**ARTICHOKE** Symbolizes the crown chakra, every leaf represents a chapter in one's life, protects the heart from emotional pain, invites passion, increases feelings of happiness

**ASPARAGUS** Fosters sex and passion, encourages truth-telling, offers protection for nature and the environment

**BEET** Used in love magick, heals broken hearts, promotes grounding and confidence, prolongs life, boosts energy and stamina, banishes enemies

**BEAN (GREEN)** Protects against anything negative, used in making decisions and choices, fosters love and marriage, increases sex and passion, encourages fertility and children, invokes money

**BROCCOLI** Offers protection from life's misfortunes, boosts energy levels, brings strength to hopeless situations

**BRUSSELS SPROUT** Cultivates happiness and stability, enhances visions, enhances beauty and confidence, offers all-around protection, boosts strength and endurance, increases courage

**CABBAGE** Improves luck and happiness, used in general protection spells, invokes money and wealth, wards off cash flow problems, alleviates unnecessary financial worries, boosts fertility, used in love magick, strengthens willpower, aids in weight loss

**CARROT** Used in fertility spells, improves sex life and sex drive, helps to connect to a higher power, encourages spiritual meditation and visions, boosts beauty and popularity

**CAULIFLOWER** Calms hot tempers, sweetens the mood of grumpy people, invokes guides and protection, settles the nerves

**CELERY** Brings about psychic visions, encourages divination, offers connection with spirits through dream-sleep, promotes concentration, helps with weight loss, aids in dealing with upsetting emotions

**CHICKPEA** Promotes pregnancy and fertility, calms the mood, enhances beauty, used in spells to strengthen and beautify the hair, aids in dealing with overwhelming emotions

**CORN** Helps bring about a change of luck, increases good fortune, offers protection from negative people or situations, promotes happiness and contentment, strengthens friendships, enhances beauty

**EGGPLANT** Encourages wisdom and knowledge, aids in discovering the truth, rejuvenates and strengthens the body, enhances sexual performance, boosts cash flow, cultivates spirituality

**GARLIC** Offers all-around protection, reverses hexes or curses, wards off illness, removes unwanted attention, boosts physical and mental strength, banishes ghosts and evil spirits, wards off thieves, fosters love and sex, wild garlic used for protecting nature and wildlife

**HORSERADISH** Wards off negativity, banishes evil spirits, boosts male sexual prowess and performance, increases fertility

**LEEK** Strengthens friendships, banishes evil, used in general health spells, offers protection from malevolent forces and protection from psychic attack

**LETTUCE** Removes fear and anxiety, sharpens psychic visions and divination, induces sleep and restfulness, attracts money and business

**MUSHROOM** Heightens psychic visions and divination, aids in protecting nature and the environment, helps with weight loss, encourages astral travel, promotes love

**ONION** Wards off unwanted visitors, banishes evil spirits, promotes luck and good fortune, casts out money worries, aids in revealing the truth, rekindles love, brings longevity to relationships

**PARSNIP** Boosts confidence and self-esteem, summons courage in confrontations, invokes money, increases wealth

**PEA** Invites love to lonely people, promotes healthy relationships and marriages, improves sex drive, used in money rituals for those who are financially struggling

**POTATO** Can be used as a poppet substitute, offers protection, used in stability spells, promotes happiness, helps in grounding oneself after divination

**PUMPKIN** Used in god and goddess worship; offers protection from evil spirits at Samhain;

good for spells to conceive, maintain wealth, and honor the moon; boosts love magick; promotes good luck; enables communication with the dead; used in fertility rituals (pumpkin seeds); enhances creative abilities; cures insomnia

**RADISH**

Red radish: Promotes love and relationships

White radish: Offers protection from the evil eye, fosters communication with spirits, invokes your guide and angels, heightens the sacral chakra

**RHUBARB** (*Note:* Only eat the stalks; the leaves are highly toxic) Boosts willpower, helps you or others overcome bad habits, keeps your lover faithful, increases male libido

**SPINACH** Increases energy, improves concentration, promotes visions and divination, enhances fertility, eases childbirth, attracts money and business.

**SWEET POTATO** Protects friendships, encourages happiness and joy, sparks communication with guides and spirits, fosters love and sex, eases stress, aids concentration

**TURNIP** For "leave me alone" spells, offers protection from negativity and protection from evil spirits at Samhain

**WATERCRESS** Used to promote psychic visions, creates harmony, brings balance and clarity to difficult situations, encourages confidence, boosts strength

## Spices

Spices don't just make food taste great, they are highly useful in the witch's pantry as well. These wonderful additions to our everyday staples have so many significant health benefits and are even more effective when incorporated in magick rituals. Witches might draw on an array of spices to make blessing oils and infusions, and they can be blended with certain blossoms and leaves to empower a spell. Incorporating them in pouches and inside of poppets is also popular. Although there are countless spices the world over, here we have included the ones most frequently used in witchcraft today. Make sure you have a good stock of these ingredients so that they are handy when you want to cast a spell.

**CARDAMOM** Can silence a gossip, entices a lover, improves sex life and libido, strengthens communication, boosts confidence when speaking in public, used for justice and a positive outcome in a court case, increases courage

**CAYENNE PEPPER (CHILI)** Used to keep a lover faithful, banishes negativity, removes hexes, clears one's mind, makes you appear more attractive to others

**CINNAMON** Burned to bless altar items, attracts money and wealth, helps to speed up the results of spells, promotes inspiration and creativity, offers protection for the home, boosts luck and victory, increases sex magick and lust

**CLOVE** Improves sexual performance, offers protection from anything dangerous, bolsters courage in difficult situations, improves memory, for charms used in love magick

**GINGER** Invokes money, spices up love affairs, boosts libido, for healing rituals, chewed to bring more energy when performing magic

**PAPRIKA** Gives spells a boost, removes curses, used in healing spells, enhances beauty within, promotes communication with a spirit

**PEPPER**

BLACK: Offers protection from evil, used in banishing spells for people and homes, removes curses, rids negativity from a place or a person

WHITE: Gets rid of obstacles, provides protection from being attacked, removes hexes, stops stalking behaviors, used in beauty spells and weight-loss rituals

**SAFFRON** Attracts partners, helps cure an obsession, for lucky amulets (dried and pressed), for a successful business, for winning a legal battle, lifts your mood, brings happiness

**STAR ANISE** Repels insects; helps you overcome insomnia, sleep disorders, and nightmares; used at Yuletide to purify spaces and altar items; thrown into open fires for protection; carried to bring luck

**TURMERIC** Used in purification rituals, improves mood, for general healing spells, used to break a spell, boosts confidence and courage

**VANILLA** Increases sex drive and passion, makes you appear more attractive to the opposite sex, calms a nervous disposition, enhances willpower and weight-loss spells, used in beauty treatments

## Easy Reference Guide

When you have a spell in mind but you're not sure which fruit, vegetable, spice, or herb to use, scan the following lists of them grouped by purpose. Remember, there are a variety of items that can work for each category, so if you find it difficult to source one, you can always substitute another one for it. Here we have also inserted additional fruits, vegetables, and spices, plus herbs (see chapter 6), that are not included in the individual entries listed on pages 184–93 and in chapter 6.

## For Banishing Evil, Overcoming Bad Habits, and Removing Negativity

Angelica • beet • blueberry • cardamom • cayenne pepper • cherry (black) • chervil • chives • clover • garlic • grapefruit • horseradish • hyssop • lemon • lemongrass • lemon verbena • nettle • onion • paprika • parsley • peach • pepper (black and white) • potato • pumpkin • saffron • St. John's wort • tomato • turnip

## For Beauty

Avocado • basil • blueberry • brussels sprout • carrot • catnip • cayenne pepper • chickpea • coconut • comfrey • corn • cucumber • lemon verbena • mandarin orange • paprika • pepper (white) • prune • vanilla

## For Concentration and Communication

Avocado ◆ blueberry ◆ cardamom ◆ cayenne pepper ◆ clove ◆ dill ◆ eggplant ◆ pomegranate ◆ pumpkin ◆ raisin ◆ sweet potato ◆ spinach

## For Confidence and Courage, Motivation, and Self-esteem

Avocado ◆ beet ◆ brussels sprout ◆ cantaloupe ◆ cardamom ◆ clove ◆ cranberry ◆ grapefruit ◆ raspberry ◆ parsley ◆ parsnip ◆ turmeric ◆ watercress

## For Creativity

Banana ◆ cinnamon ◆ grapefruit ◆ hyssop ◆ lemon ◆ orange ◆ pineapple ◆ pumpkin

## For Divination and Psychic Awareness

Arnica ◆ basil ◆ bay leaf ◆ blueberry ◆ brussels sprout ◆ celery ◆ chamomile ◆ cherry ◆ cinnamon ◆ date ◆ elderberry ◆ grape (purple) ◆ grapefruit ◆ lettuce ◆ lychee ◆ mushroom ◆ mugwort ◆ orange ◆ passion fruit ◆ potato ◆ radish ◆ spinach

## For Emotional Balance

Apricot ◆ artichoke ◆ avocado ◆ basil ◆ beet ◆ bergamot ◆ cauliflower ◆ celery ◆ cherry ◆ chervil ◆ chickpea ◆ comfrey ◆ elderberry ◆ feverfew ◆ grapefruit ◆ lemon ◆ lemongrass ◆ lemon verbena ◆ lettuce ◆ lime ◆ orange

• passion fruit • pineapple • saffron • St. John's wort • strawberry • sweet potato • turmeric • vanilla • watermelon

## For Fertility and Family

Apricot • arnica • avocado • basil • bean (green) • blackberry • cabbage • carrot • chickpea • grape • grapefruit • lemongras • lovage • olive • orange • peach • pumpkin • quince • raspberry • spinach

## For Fidelity

Cayenne pepper • coconut • elderberry • passion fruit

## For Friendships

Avocado • catnip • corn • leek • lime • lovage • mandarin orange • sweet potato

## For Happiness and Change

Apple • artichoke • avocado • banana • borage • brussels sprout • catnip • cabbage • cantaloupe • chamomile • clover • corn • feverfew • grapefruit • kiwi • lychee • mandarin orange • olive • peach • pineapple • potato • quince • raspberry • sweet potato • oregano • saffron

## For Health and Healing

Aloe vera • bergamot • chamomile • chervil • chives • chicory • comfrey • dill • eucalyptus • echinacea • fennel • feverfew • frankincense • garlic

• ginger • ginseng root • lavender • lemon balm • lemon grass • mint • parsley • paprika • sandalwood • St. John's wort • tea tree • turmeric

## For Houses and Homes

Borage • cinnamon • coconut • lemon • pepper (black and white) • star anise

## For Intellect and Learning

Ginkgo biloba • ginger • kale (and other leafy greens) • lemon balm • pepper (black) • peppermint • rosemary • turmeric

## For Legal Matters

Cardamom • dill • saffron

## For Love, Sex, and Relationships

Apple • apricot • artichoke • asparagus • avocado • banana • basil • blueberry • beet • bean (green) • cabbage • cardamom • carrot • cherry • cinnamon • clove • coconut • cranberry • date • echinacea • eggplant • garlic • ginger • grape (green) • horseradish • kiwi • lemongrass • lovage • lychee • mushroom • olive • onion • orange • oregano • parsley • pea • peach • pear • pineapple • plum • pomegranate • prune • pumpkin • quince • radish • raisin • raspberry • rhubarb • saffron • strawberry • sweet potato • tomato • vanilla • watercress • watermelon

## For Luck, Success, and New Beginnings

Banana • basil • cabbage • cinnamon • clover • dill • fenugreek • grape (green) • kiwi • onion • pineapple • raspberry • star anise • tomato • watermelon

## For Money and Work

Banana • basil • bay • bean (green) • blackberry • borage • chicory • cinnamon • comfrey • clover • eggplant • fenugreek • ginger • grape (green) • lettuce • ime • mint • orange • onions • oregano • parsley • parsnip • peas • pear • pineapple • plum • spinach • sorrel • tomato

## For Nature, Animals, and the Environment

Arnica • asparagus • avocado • catnip • garlic • lemon • nettle • sorrel • star anise

## For Protection

Angelica • arnica • bay • basil • blackberry • broccoli • bean (green) • brussels sprout • cabbage • cantaloupe • chives • cinnamon • clove • coconut • comfrey • corn • dill • elderberry • feverfew • garlic • hyssop • leek • lemon verbena • lime • mandarin orange • mint • mugwort • nettle • oregano • peach • pepper (black and white) • pomegranate • potato • quince • radish • star anise • tomato • turnip

## For Sleep, Insomnia, and Nightmares

Catnip • cherry • chive • kiwi • lettuce • lavender • mandarin orange • plum • prune • star anise

## For Spiritual Connection and Meditation

Angelica • arnica • banana • brussels sprout • cantaloupe • cauliflower • carrot • celery • chamomile • cherry • date • eggplant • elderberry • fennel • grapes • holy basil • hyssop purple • mint • mugwort • mushroom • orange • paprika • pomegranate • pumpkin • quince • radish • sweet potato • watermelon

## For Strength, Vigor, and Courage

Banana • bay leaf • beet • borage • broccoli • brussel sprouts • cardamom • cranberry • date • echinacea • eggplant • fennel • garlic • grape (red) • grapefruit • lime • lychee • parsley • spinach

## For Willpower and Weight Loss

Avocado • blueberry • catnip • cabbage • celery • chicory • chive • fenugreek • ginger • lemon • mushroom • oregano • peach • pear • pepper (white) • raisin • rhubarb • tomato • vanilla

Chapter 8

# Essential and Magickal Natural Oils

WHEN YOU SET ABOUT MAKING YOUR MAGICKAL OILS, pay attention to how you are feeling. If you want your blends to work perfectly, you must be in a good mood—so if you woke up grumpy or headachy, leave it for another day. You'll be projecting your positive influence over the oils so make sure you won't be disturbed while blending and don't let your mind drift to other things. The best magickal ingredients are usually found in your pantry. A few drops of this and pinches of that often make for the perfect recipe. Most witches were probably witches in another life, so your soul might already know the best way to do it. Trust your instincts: there's no right or wrong way—remember this is your oil, you're in charge, and it will be just fine!

# MAKING YOUR OWN ANOINTING OILS

Whenever you set about performing a ritual that requires anointing a candle or a crystal, using home-blended oils is the best way to go. You must start by sourcing a base oil. Vegetable oil, canola oil, sunflower oil, or olive oil is suitable. If you would like guidance on the specific magickal correspondences of various fruits, vegetables, herbs, and spices, refer to the Easy Reference Guide on pages 194–99 in this book, where you can see which ingredients you can use to infuse the oil. You really don't need a large amount of infusing material in a recipe. For instance, if you were making an herb-infused oil in a 10 ml bottle (about the size of a bottle of essential oil), a few pinches of each herb would suffice.

This magickal oil will hold its power for about three months; after this, the magick will start to wane. If you don't have space to grow your own herbs, you can purchase little bags of many different varieties online. As we mentioned earlier, there are many witches with surplus amounts of dried herbs, so they will sell them happily for a few dollars a bag. If you do order them, be sure to perform a blessing over the herbs when they arrive. You can do this by transferring the herbs to a bowl and saying a short affirmation, like *I bless these herbs, let their magick infuse with mine*. Get a selection of small mason jars to store the herbs in, and keep them—and the oils—in a cool, dark, dry place.

A basic, uninfused oil works as a good all-purpose anointing oil for crystals and candles; this will bless the items on your altar and work well if you want to perform a spell quickly (see below for instructions). However, if you have time, try to opt for an anointing oil that corresponds with the task at hand and uses the herbs associated with the spell you want to cast. For instance, if you are spellcasting for better sleep, rather than using just a basic anointing oil, it will have more power if you use oil infused with lavender. But you can also be creative when blending and using magickal oils, and if a specific ingredient is calling to you, go with the "feels right" theory.

## Blessing Your Oils

Whether you are using a basic or custom-infused oil, it is important to cast a general blessing over the oil during the blending process. To make a basic anointing oil, no herbs are needed: simply pour vegetable, canola, sunflower, or olive oil into a small bottle. For an infused oil, mix your ingredients and the oil in a glass jar. Leave the lid off the bottle or jar throughout the duration of the spell.

Light a white candle beside the bottle or jar and say this blessing once over the oil:

***"I cleanse this oil, now free from impurity.<br>I bless this oil, infused with love.<br>I call for assistance to empower my magick,<br>I welcome the Goddess / Angels from above.<br>So mote it be."***

It's always best to let the candle burn down (attended, of course), so use a small 4-inch (10 cm) spell candle or a tealight; you can then transfer your oil into bottle(s) or if you are using a jar, screw the lid on.

If you are making a basic oil, you might want to make a batch all at once. These pre-blessed bottles can be used as a base oil for any more intricate blends you choose to make in the future. As always, store the oils in a cool, dark, dry place.

## How to Anoint

To anoint a candle, simply dab a little oil onto your finger and smear it down the full length of the candle before you light it.

For crystal anointing, place a few drops of oil onto the stone and massage it in.

You can also anoint other items on your altar this way, such as an athame, a chalice, or even the altar surface itself. Just make sure that the object you are anointing won't be damaged (such as certain types of porous crystals) when it comes into contact with the oil.

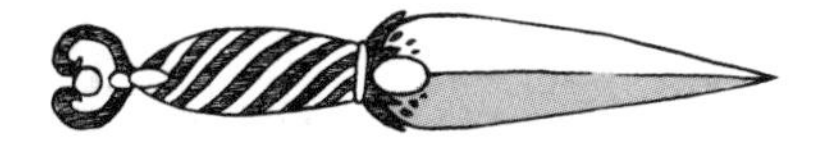

On the following pages are some ideas on different kinds of anointing oils. You might not be able to source some of the herbs, but you can always substitute one by referring to the Easy Reference Guide on pages 194–99.

## Oil to Banish Negativity

Sometimes, negative energy clings to us, especially if we have been going through a rough time or if we have been feeling unhappy. Energy is contagious, so once it takes hold it can be difficult to rid yourself of it. If you are performing a spell to cast out negativity from your life, this one is a great cleanser and will spiritually disinfect you and any area the oil comes into contact with.

### MATERIALS

- 2 fresh chive stems, chopped into tiny pieces
- 1 dried sage leaf, crumbled or chopped
- A glass jar
- 2 teaspoons (10 ml) extra-virgin olive oil (pre-blessed oil will boost the spell, see page pages 202–3)
- 5 drops frankincense essential oil
- 1 white tealight candle
- A tea strainer
- Mini funnel
- 10 ml glass bottle with screw-top lid

### RITUAL

On a new moon phase, place the chopped chives and sage leaves in the glass jar and pour the olive oil on top. Sprinkle 5 drops of the frankincense oil and mix well. Light your candle, bless it by saying this chant:

*"I charge this oil with all things positive.
All negative vibes shall be gone."*

Let the candle burn down (attended), and then let the mixture steep for three days.

Strain the oil through a tea strainer and use a funnel to transfer it into a 10 ml glass bottle with a screw top. Screw the lid on. Don't throw away the contents of the tea strainer; they can be scattered outside your front door afterward to give you added protection from anything untoward.

## Other Uses for Oil to Banish Negativity

- Anoint candles or crystals with the oil before spellcasting.
- Dab a few drops on your wrist every morning to repel negativity.
- Dip your finger in the oil and massage into the dashboard of your car for stress-free driving.
- Smear around the door jambs to keep negative people from entering your home.
- If you have a negative in-law who doesn't like you, purchase some potpourri and drizzle a little of the oil over the dried contents. Place the potpourri in a pretty bowl and give it to them as a gift. Their mood should sweeten.
- Add a few drops to your bathwater to clear away stuck energy from your aura.
- To overcome bad habits, massage a few drops into your hands every day.

## Oil for Psychic and Divination Work

Whenever you want to connect with a higher power or enhance your psychic abilities, this oil serves as a carrier to otherworldly dimensions, clearing away earthly obstacles and raising your vibration. Bless the basic oil before you start and then follow the instructions below.

### MATERIALS

2 teaspoons (10 ml) canola oil (pre-blessed oil will boost the spell, see pages 202–3)

Small pinch of fennel seeds

Pinch of chamomile seeds

Pinch of dried mugwort

2 pieces of quartz crystal chips (tiny pieces)

A glass jar

A purple candle

Mini funnel

10 ml glass bottle with screw-top lid

### RITUAL

On any moon phase, mix all the ingredients (through the crystal chips) in a glass jar and leave the mixture to infuse overnight. The next morning, light a purple candle beside the oil and say this chant three times:

*"I bless this oil, infused with powers,*
*To connect with spirit in the nighttime hours."*

Once you have recited the spell, close by saying the words, "So mote it be."

When the candle has burned down, strain the oil and use the funnel to carefully transfer the oil and the contents into the 10 ml glass bottle and screw on the lid.

## Other Uses for Oil for Psychic and Divination Work

- To connect with your chosen deity, anoint your altar by smearing a little of the oil onto the surface (one drop is enough).
- To enhance your psychic vision, rub a little onto your temples.*
- Heat some of the oil in an infuser and burn while you are performing any readings.
- To improve prophetic dreams, leave the open bottle by the bedside overnight.
- For profound meditations, add a few drops to the bathwater and bathe in it before meditating.*

* *Note:* Oil containing mugwort should not be used if you are pregnant or breastfeeding; it also might cause skin allergies so patch-test a small area before use and wait 24 hours.

# Protection Oil

Everyone should always have at least one bottle of protection oil ready and available at all times. There are numerous recipes for protection oils online, but this one is quite versatile and works exceptionally well if used alongside tourmaline.

## MATERIALS

- 2 teaspoons (10 ml) extra-virgin olive oil (pre-blessed oil will boost the spell, see pages 202–3)
- ½ garlic clove, peeled and chopped
- 3 small pieces dried angelica root
- Pinch of dried basil
- 3 drops myrrh essential oil
- 3 tourmaline crystal chips (tiny pieces)
- A glass jar
- A small black candle
- A small white candle
- Mini funnel
- 10 ml glass bottle with screw-top lid

## RITUAL

It's essential to fully infuse the oil with the crystal chips, so on a full moon phase, simply mix the olive oil, garlic, herbs, myrrh essential oil, and tourmaline chips in a glass jar and leave it outdoors (or on a moonlit windowsill) on a dry night to soak up the moon's rays.

The following day, you can add even more magick by lighting one black candle and one white candle next to the oil. While the candles are burning, visualize the black candle capturing anything harmful or dangerous and the white candle bathing you in protection. Once they have burned down (attended), you can strain the oil and use a funnel to transfer the contents into a 10 ml glass bottle.

## Other Uses for Protection Oil

- Anoint candles or crystals for spells that involve protection.
- Smear a few drops of the oil around all the doorframes in your home.
- If you want to protect a child, rub the oil on the child's backpack.
- For protection when driving, rub a few drops into each wheel of the car once a month. You can also saturate a small piece of fabric with the oil and place it in the car's glove compartment.
- To protect yourself, dab a little oil onto clothing.
- To protect someone else, anoint and light a white candle next to a photograph of the person on your altar. Dab a little oil on the picture as well.

# Lucky Oil

This oil needs to be made when life is throwing you one problem after another. Performing it on a new moon can turn around your fortune, casting out any negativity and setting you on a lucky streak.

**MATERIALS**

A white tealight candle

Oil burner

2 teaspoons (10 ml) olive oil (pre-blessed oil will boost the spell, see pages 202–3)

1 whole star anise

¼ teaspoon cinnamon powder

Pinch of dried dill

A tea strainer

A glass jar

Mini funnel

10 ml glass bottle with screw-top lid

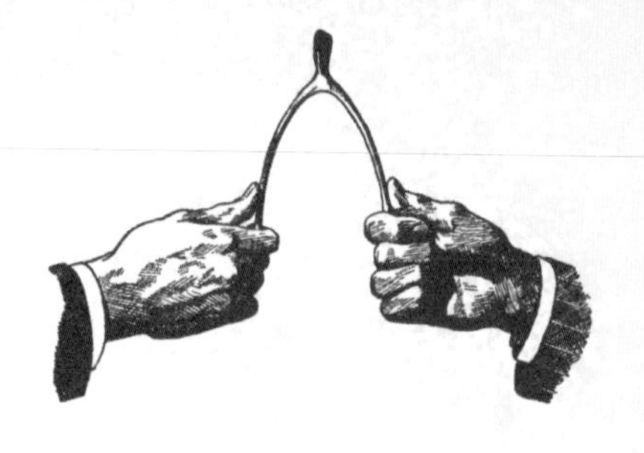

**RITUAL**

Light a white tealight candle under the well of the oil burner. Add the olive oil and herbs to the well, and heat up the ingredients until the oil is warm, about 30 minutes. While it is heating, speak this chant twelve times:

*"I will arrange my luck to change, from here on in, good things begin."*

When you have said the chant, close with the words "So mote it be."

Snuff out the candle and strain the oil through a tea strainer into a glass jar. Carefully pick out the star anise, wipe it off, and set it aside. Using a funnel, transfer the oil into the 10 ml glass bottle with a screw-top lid (leaving the lid off) and relight the tealight until it burns down (attended). Screw on the lid.

Keep the star anise in your wallet for a few months; this will increase your finances and ensure that luck will be directed your way.

## Other Lucky Oil Uses

- To change your luck from bad to good, add a few drops of the oil to some food before cooking.
- For more money luck, anoint a piece of sunstone with the oil and place the crystal on a windowsill in your home.

- Anoint a blue candle with the oil before going on job interviews.
- If you are taking an exam, make sure you have the star anise with you. You can sew it into the hem of your clothing or put it in a locket around your neck.
- If you are taking a driving test, anoint a piece of amazonite or rose quartz crystal with the oil and carry it with you.
- For luck in love, dab a few drops on your skin every day, just above your heart. (*Note*: Patch-test your skin first for 24 hours, as cinnamon can be irritating to certain people.)

## Healing Oil

Creating your own healing oils can be done with a variety of herbs. There are countless herbs and many different recipes that you can research in books and on the internet. For specific physical ailments, though, it is best to consult your health-care provider first before using essential oils, so we are focusing here on a more all-around magickal healing spell.

If you want to send general healing energy to another person, or cast spells for general well-being, this recipe works very well.

### MATERIALS

2 teaspoons (10 ml) vegetable oil (pre-blessed oil will boost the spell, see pages 202–3)

2 drops bergamot oil

2 drops sandalwood oil

2 drops tea tree oil

A glass jar

A small yellow or gold candle

A sandalwood incense stick

2 large white candles

Mini funnel

10 ml glass bottle with screw-top lid

**RITUAL**

On the evening of a waning moon, blend the oils in a glass jar and set up your altar, placing the oil, the yellow or gold candle, and the sandalwood incense stick in the center, and the two large white candles at the back on either side. Light the candles and burn the sandalwood incense. Say this blessing seven times:

*"This healing oil will make all well,*
*With the magick I make with this spell."*

When you have said the blessing, close with the words "So mote it be."

When the incense has burned down, add the sandalwood ashes to the oil and stir them in well. When the candles have burned down (do not leave them unattended), your oil will be ready. Use the funnel to transfer it into the 10 ml glass bottle and screw on the lid.

## Other Healing Oil Uses

- For general healing, anoint any candles or crystals with the oil prior to beginning the ritual.
- When performing a healing spell, place a picture of the sufferer on the altar and dab a little of the oil onto the face of the individual in the photo.

- For those who suffer from insomnia, replace all ingredients with 2 drops of both lavender and chamomile oil and dab a few drops around the bed frame and on each temple. (*Note*: Please check precautions first, though, with your health-care provider; many herbs should not come in contact with skin for people with certain conditions.)
- To use any kind of healing oil, you can add a few drops to the bathwater, massage it into your temples, burn ten drops in an oil burner with water, or anoint the third-eye chakra daily. (See the note above on skin precautions.)

## Banishing Oil

Witches use banishing oil much like protection oil. Rather than shielding yourself from negativity, for banishments you are getting rid of something harmful and insisting it never come back. These oils are commonly used in hauntings to remove a property of spirits, for stopping stalkers, or for casting away drug dealers or people who have an unhealthy influence in your life. We've even known witches who use it to spur problematic neighbors to move away.

You can eradicate anything with a strong mind and a forceful attitude, so if your oil is going to be successful, you really need to mean what you are saying and be confident in your actions. If it's a person you wish to banish, you need to take care and make sure that you are not inadvertently sending him or her negative energy. Spells like this can sometimes go horribly wrong, and you could send them a dose of something nasty that could, in turn, bounce right back to you. For example, if you want to get your neighbor to move out of the vicinity, you would project your intent in a positive way, asking for them to find their dream house. Keep your thoughts neutral, and when you banish someone, wish them well and send them love. That's not always easy if you are dealing with an especially difficult person, but you have to rise above your emotions and not allow yourself to send them any unpleasant thoughts.

## MATERIALS

2 teaspoons (10 ml) extra-virgin olive oil (pre-blessed oil will boost the spell, see pages 202–3)

½ clove garlic, finely chopped

Pinch of mugwort

Pinch of cayenne pepper

Pinch of dried sage or 1 fresh sage leaf

A glass jar

7 white tealight candles

Photograph of the person(s) you wish to banish (not required, but helpful) or a piece of paper with their name(s) on it

Mini funnel

10 ml glass bottle with screw-top lid

## RITUAL

On a full moon, mix together the oil, garlic, and herbs in a glass jar. Place the jar on your altar and light the seven tealight candles; place them in a circle around the jar.

If you are able to obtain a photograph of the person(s), rest it on the front of your altar; if not, use the piece of paper with their name on it. Anoint the photograph or paper with the oil (take care not to put it too close to the candles). Say this chant twelve times:

*"I summon protective magick this day,*
*Cast all bad out, let all good stay."*

When you have said the chant, close by saying, "So mote it be."

When the candles have burned down (do not leave them unattended), your oil will be ready. Use the funnel to transfer it into the 10 ml glass bottle, and screw on the lid.

## Other Banishing Oil Uses

- Anoint all candles with Banishing Oil prior to a banishing ritual.
- If someone is stalking you, dab a little of the oil on to the hem of your clothing when you're out and about.
- Smear the oil around the doorframes in your home to deter unwanted people from entering.
- To rid a home of ghosts, mix ten drops of the oil with one cup (237 ml) of rainwater or spring water. Transfer the mixture to a plastic spray bottle and squirt around all the floors in your home.
- And finally, to move that neighbor on, sprinkle some oil on a neighboring fence or pathway; or if you're in an apartment, on a shared wall.

Part Three

# Holistic Home, Garden, and Family

## Chapter 9

# The Enchanted House and Garden

**DO YOU HAVE A GREEN THUMB OR ARE YOU ALL THUMBS** when it comes to keeping plants alive? Whatever your past experience with growing and nurturing plants, flowers, trees, and other greenery, this chapter will give you ideas that you can work with.

For witches who are lucky enough to have a garden, however big or small, you can create a magickal space with meaning. Many Wiccans love nature and like nothing more than being at one with the environment, growing, nurturing, and tending to their land. Keen, witchy gardeners will grow flowers and shrubs that possess a magickal significance and plant trees that bring harmony and prosperity to the people who reside there. When we look at the phases of a female witch—"Maiden, Mother, and Crone"—we often find that witches become more enamored of gardening in their Mother/Crone phase of life, meaning that once the female witch matures, she begins to take a more avid interest in all kinds of plant life. Some Maiden witches who are more highly evolved souls also take pleasure from growing plants and nurturing fauna. You can spot these types very early when they are children: they will putter around with their parents and show delight at unearthing the first harvest of potatoes or become obsessed with worms, butterflies, and other garden insects.

## COMMON GARDEN PLANTS THAT BOOST MAGICKAL ENERGY

You can easily bring magick and positive energy into your home or yard with plants that are readily available; in fact, you might already have a few of them lurking at the edges of your property!

### Cowslip (*Primula veris*)

These outdoor lovelies are steeped in ancient English folklore and were associated with fairies. It was believed that around the time of Beltane (May Day), cowslips would ward off pesky fairies, and the plants were often strewn over the threshold for protection. In later folklore, it was thought that fairies would hide inside the flowers to protect themselves

from danger. Cowslips are found growing in pastures and meadows, but many witches like to plant them in garden borders. Their delicate yellow flowers hang downward, resembling a cluster of keys, meaning that the plant can expose secrets and find hidden things. For spellcraft, you can dry the flowers and use them in rituals when you want to reveal the truth.

## **Daisy** (*Bellis perennis*, common daisy, or *Leucanthemum vulgare*, oxeye daisy)

Sweet, sweet daisies, with their happy little faces! They bring joy simply by being. Daisies are deceptive—because they're so prevalent, they're often overlooked as being too common to be truly special. But daisies are persistent and adaptable. They pop up wherever they feel like growing, and sometimes appear where you wouldn't believe anything could grow. Even when they start to look tattered by rain and weather, they're still cheerful. In the Middle Ages, the humble daisy was used for love divination—this is the derivation of the old saying *"He [or she, or they] loves me, he [or she, or they] loves me not"*—and because of this, these charming flowers are often used in love spells to reveal the feelings of a potential lover.

The daisy also encourages us to recognize that modesty and an unassuming nature are wondrous attributes—precisely what the world around us needs today. Make yourself a crown of daisies and wear it while you meditate and give thanks for your unique qualities.

## **Foxglove** (*Digitalis*)

However stunning these ornamental beauties are, all parts of foxgloves are highly poisonous and can be fatal if ingested. This plant is just as toxic for cats and dogs, but our pets must have a hidden knowledge of this because they usually steer clear of foxglove when they are running around in the garden. Because of its potential deadly properties, it is no wonder that foxglove was steeped in magick for centuries. Formerly, herbalists would extract parts of the plant to use in their medicines, but nowadays, you should not use any part of foxglove for self-medication. There is a prescription heart medication, though, digoxin, that is made from chemicals extracted from the plant. Like the cowslip, foxglove is associated with fairies, so whenever one of these showy blooms pops up in the border, it means your garden is likely alive with nature sprites.

## **Honeysuckle** (*Lonicera*)

Most witches who are lucky enough to have a garden will try to grow honeysuckle. These plants with their delicate tubular flowers are money magnets; they can also enhance your intuition and help out when you are trying to develop your psychic abilities. When the plant is flowering, remove some of the leaves and dry them on a tray for a few weeks. Once dried, scrunch them up and place them on your altar whenever you are performing a wealth spell. You can also mix them with salt and aventurine chips to enhance their power.

## Jasmine (*Jasminum*)

Witches love this plant because it has so many magickal uses. Not only does it promote peace and protection, it is also used in spell pouches and jars to attract love into someone's life. Burning the flowers in a bedroom (in a fireproof dish) before sleep encourages mediumistic dreams and connections to the spirit world. It is also grown in gardens to entice fairies and nature spirits. Having quartz crystals nearby, either buried in the plant's soil or carried in a pouch along with dried jasmine flowers, will help to inspire creative types. Every witch who has a garden must try to grow some jasmine. They have such a heady scent that on a breezy day, you can smell it everywhere.

Jasmine is powerful when used in any healing spells, and the flowers can be entwined into decorative broomsticks to give the besom more magick.

## **Lavender** (*Lavendula*)

Lavender always comes up as a top choice for any magickal garden precisely because it has such a grounded and calming influence. Lavender tends to tolerate even poor soil and questionable watering practices. It spreads from year to year, so your initial plantings will take off and provide more and more flowers as time goes by.

You can take lavender cuttings and place them in a footbath. Breathe in the soothing scent of the leaves as you let yourself relax or hang dried bunches in the windows of your home to generate calm and peaceful energy. For the ultimate experience, set up an area outside where you can revel in nature while allowing the lavender to smooth out any stressful edges of your day. Also see pages 116–17 for more information on lavender aromatherapy and magick.

## **Raspberry** (*Rubus*)

The raspberry plant is all about encouraging us to explore the spiritual and look within ourselves to evaluate what we are (or aren't) doing. In times past, when someone in the household died, the plant would be cut back and the branches placed on the front door. This would ensure that the spirit of the deceased could not reenter the home and would have a safe passage to the spirit world. Later folklore tells us that a small branch should be carried by a pregnant woman to ease labor pains and ensure a healthy pregnancy. And because of the fruit's red color, raspberries were often substituted in rituals that required blood use.

Today, it is included in love magick to keep a lover faithful and strengthen and recharge relationships.

## Rose (*Rosa*)

It is not uncommon to see roses growing in most well-kept gardens, but what many don't realize is that they are one of the most magickal plants in spellcraft and can be used in countless ways to improve your life. Regardless of the color of the rose, these impressive blooms are traditionally associated with love and passion. You can dry the petals for love spells to either entice a new mate or to keep relationships sweet. The thorns of the plant should be carefully removed and placed in a "witch bottle"—a bottle that will hold a protection spell to guard your household.

## Sunflower (*Helianthus*)

These tall, hardy plants with blazing yellow flowers are often grown next to moonflowers—the common name for several species of night-blooming plants with white flowers—to represent the sun and the moon being in sync with the earth. Because the sunflower's ring of petals also looks similar to a lion's mane, it is no coincidence that witches use them in magick for strength and courage. There is nothing more spectacular than seeing a row of these giant beauties, and, when planted in groups, they will supercharge your garden, bringing happiness and fertility to the land.

# Plant Parenthood—Leanna

Many years ago, when I was young and naive, my mother came to visit me for a week. I heard her gasp as I followed her into my conservatory. On the long windowsill were four of the unfortunate specimens that I had forgotten to water, and, sadly, they had passed over to plant heaven.

My mother, who is ordinarily quite laid-back, was very upset; it was one of those rare times in my life when she told me off, good and proper. "Who else is there to care for them if you don't do it?" she said, and "How would you have liked it if I'd kept you without a drink!" She went on to inform me that plants are like children and that they have feelings. Although at the time I thought that she was completely overreacting, as I have matured, I can only hang my head in shame.

The lecture she gave me on plant care—including watering and feeding schedules—and compost improvement has set me in good stead. I have since learned to tune into the sensitivity of these growing wonders and am a houseplant fanatic. I even taught my son the same principles and he is now a professional gardener. What is so lovely is that we are often outdoors together, growing all sorts of plants and vegetables, so we can share in our green-thumbed enthusiasm.

# INDOOR PLANTS

Whether you're moving into a new home or you've been in your place for twenty years, you can increase and enhance the positive energy in your space with specific plants. Some of these have been used for good luck since ancient times, so you are drawing on the wisdom of millennia when you make an orchid or lucky bamboo the centerpiece of a room or a ritual. All these plants are grown in containers, so they can easily be incorporated into even the smallest of spaces. And adding a plant to any room is like giving it an instant makeover—suddenly, it's fresh, crisp, and full of life!

The plants we have in our home play a mysterious role in our lives, as they emit unique energy that can affect our mood and the good fortune we might attract. Witches are known for loving their indoor plants and flowers, and will often take time to tune into each and every one of their needs. Because plants are alive, we have to give them respect and care; talking to them softly and kindly has been scientifically proved to help them grow better. Like any other living thing, they respond.

## Lucky Bamboo (*Dracaena sanderiana*)

The name of this plant says it all! Lucky bamboo plants are typically sold as small arrangements of stalks in a container with pebbles or stones (or sometimes dirt) and a small amount of water. Lucky bamboo carries wise energy and shows us to how be open (as its stalks are hollow), flexible, and persistent. It encourages peaceful and humble growth, and brings prosperity. Many bamboo plants that you see in stores have curved or braided stalks, but this is not how the plant grows in nature.

Bamboo is often used in feng shui, the Chinese practice of aligning the energetic forces of a living space with the people who reside in it. It incorporates the elements of wood, metal, earth, water, and fire, and prescribes certain sectors of the home where each element works best.

According to feng shui, the number of stalks in a bamboo plant are also symbolic:

- Two stalks of bamboo bring love, marriage, and companionship.
- Three stalks foster peace, happiness, and wealth.
- Four stalks are unlucky, so avoid arranging four stalks together.
- Five stalks can improve health conditions.
- Six or nine stalks attract good fortune and extra cash.

To keep your lucky bamboo plant thriving for years, make sure to add only an inch of water to the base of the container, and change the water weekly. Don't expose it to direct sunlight, but do turn the plant weekly, as the stalks at the back of the pot will reach for the sun. Fertilize it once a month with a rather diluted solution.

## **Cactus** (Any variety)

Most cactus plants look prickly, but grown in the home they actually create wonderful energy and are believed to capture and expel unhappiness and anxiety. Cacti need very little care or watering and are thought to remove harmful electromagnetic waves, especially if you place one near your computer when you are working.

## Chinese Money Plant (*Pilea peperomiodes*)

Not to be confused with what is commonly called the money tree (*Pachira aquatica*), the Chinese money plant or pancake plant has fat, shiny, round leaves that resemble large coins. Legend has it that if a money plant thrives in your home, you will never be short of cash. It will bring joy, happiness, and abundance. They are not only lucky, they are also helpful if you've been feeling a little down in the dumps. If you know someone who is a bit down on their luck, give one as a gift, and their life will soon improve. Most people keep them as houseplants, but they can sometimes survive outside in a garden or on a terrace in a warm climate.

This is another plant that is used to promote good feng shui. Experts say that placing it in front of a sharp corner in the home will eliminate stress and worry. The money plant also helps to reduce arguments and bring about a good night's sleep. This makes it a nice purifying plant, and a good choice for a bedroom or anywhere you like to rest and relax.

Money plants like a humid environment and sandy, well-drained soil. They can tolerate moist soil but be careful not to overwater them—this can lead to root rot and the demise of your lucky green friend! You can place this plant in a sunny spot, as it can tolerate full sun for at least part of the day.

## Chrysanthemum (*Chrysanthemum*)

Also known as mums, these lush flowers were first cultivated in ancient China, and the flower is an integral part of the culture of both China and Japan. Both the flowers and the leaves, dried, work brilliantly if you want to banish something or someone from your life. The chrysanthemum emits protective vibrations, so place a potted one by your front door. These plants are also helpful in spells when you want to ward off family arguments or if tensions are running high between partners.

## Jade Plant (*Crassula ovata*)

This is a must-have plant for the home, especially if you want to keep your cash flowing nicely (it is also one of several species known as a "money plant" or a "money tree"). Jade is a lovely succulent with small, round, fat leaves that represent growth and new, positive energy. The leaves look a little like small jade stones, which are a symbol of wealth and success. A jade plant is traditionally given to the owners of a business as a gift, and placed near the entrance to their shop or office. However, you can situate it in your own home office or near the front door of your home to bring prosperous energy into your space. Feng shui experts recommend placing a jade plant in a southeast location of a home or business for a grounded energy that invites continued success.

A flowering jade plant signifies strong friendships or love, blessings, and continued success. Try combining jade and a Chinese money plant in the same area to boost good fortune and resilience in love, life, and business matters.

Jade is a great option for those of us who have trouble keeping plants alive! Succulents are easy to care for, as they need little watering. In fact, you shouldn't water jade until the soil feels dry to the touch. These plants need full sun to thrive, so keep this in mind when you choose its permanent location, or put it on a sunny windowsill for a good part of the day.

Finally, just make sure your jade plant has a nice big pot and don't let it dry out. If you do decide to have one of these in the home, for the magick to work it is vital that you tie a bright red ribbon in a bow loosely around one of the stems. You can take cuttings for your friends and pass on the good fortune.

## **Orchid** (*Orchidaceae* family)

Orchids are an excellent value, as they last so long and can be pruned to stimulate a batch of new blossoms, which usually appear after six months or so. Perhaps the most delicate of all houseplants, orchids are a symbol of ultimate luxury: pure beauty that must be properly cared for, lest it fades before your very eyes.

In ancient Greece, orchids were a sign of virility and fertility. (In fact, the word orchid comes from the Greek word for testicles, órchis, because of the testicle-like shape of the paired tubers of some species.) If a man wanted to sire a son, he consumed large orchid tubers. On the other hand, if a woman wanted to give birth to a girl, she ate small orchid tubers.

Orchids are regarded as sexy flowers because they represent virility, fertility, and passion. Witches love them in the home, particularly moth orchids, as they are said to keep romance alive and bring faithfulness to their relationship. Keep a potted orchid plant on your altar whenever you want to weave love magick or if you are having trouble conceiving.

Bringing an orchid into your home can also promote various types of energy. Generally speaking, orchids represent love, beauty, strength, success, and refinement. Some orchid energies are more specific, depending on their color:

- **YELLOW** New beginnings, friendship, and happiness
- **PURPLE** Royalty, dignity, and respect
- **RED** Passion, desire, and courage
- **PINK** Happiness, peace, and grace
- **WHITE** Innocence, purity, and humility
- **ORANGE** Boldness, excitement, and pure delight

Because orchids represent the entire spectrum of spirituality, you can use them in any kind of ceremony or meditation. Their exquisiteness can be a source of inspiration for a love spell, for example. Write the name of your beloved on the side of a red taper candle. (Use a pen or pencil and etch the name right into the wax.) Light the candle and allow it to burn for a minute or two. Take a small piece of an orchid petal and place it on a plate. Drip the wax from the red candle onto the petal while envisioning you and your love in a perfect embrace. Draw a deep breath and say aloud:

*"I see my perfect relationship in my mind's eye, and I trust that Spirit will bring it to me. So mote it be."*

Orchids need a warm room with bright light but not direct sunlight, which can damage their leaves. If the leaves of your plant turn reddish, this means it's getting too much sun. If the leaves are dark, it's not getting enough light. Water your plant once a week early in the morning so that the plant has time to absorb the water through the brightest and warmest part of the day.

Many people will fertilize the soil with used coffee grounds, which is beneficial to the plant. Although these plants are stunning to look at, regularly check for little white mealy bugs that can decimate and kill them. An orchid is best watered once a week under a running tap and drained well before you take it back to its original place. Daily misting is also recommended.

## Peace Lily (*Spathiphyllum*)

The peace lily is another fine choice for anyone who doesn't necessarily have a green thumb. It grows well in both shade and artificial light, which means you can bring it into your office or an area of your home with no windows and it will still thrive. It is beautiful to look at, with white flowers and dark green foliage. The energy from this plant also encourages prosperity and virtue, and adds a layer of spiritual protection. This is a nice plant to add to a space that needs some calming, such as a chaotic office, or a home where stress or emotions are running high.

Use the peace lily as a touchstone when negative emotions begin to swirl at home or at work. Take a moment to sit with this plant, taking some deep breaths in its presence. Visualize breathing in the pure filtered air it offers, and imagine it taking in the old, damaged energy from the space and converting it to a renewed source of life. When you're finished with your calming moment, offer thanks to the peace lily for its tranquil presence.

This plant prefers low lighting, moist soil, and misting. It responds well to a cool—but not cold—room, and, as the name suggests, it generates a peaceful and positive ambience. Have one of these nearby whenever you are casting spells to alleviate tension. A leaf or two can also be used dried and crushed and infused in anointing oils for peace and happiness.

## Snake Plant (*Dracaena trifasciata*)

This popular houseplant, also known as "mother-in-law's-tongue" or "viper's bowstring hemp," has thick, spiky green leaves and is a perfect specimen for beginner witches, as it needs very little care. Keeping one of these in the home is encouraged: not only does it remove excessive amounts of carbon monoxide from its surroundings, but it also absorbs negativity. Witches also use the snake plant in spells to heighten intelligence or to attract prosperity.

This plant does best in bright, indirect light; allow the soil to dry between watering to avoid root rot.

## WITCHY KITCHEN GARDENING

Although I (Leanna) consider myself an eclectic witch, I have to say that I also lean very much toward kitchen witchery and gardening. There's nothing better than spending a few hours in the kitchen boiling up potions and making blended oils for my spellcraft.

I have a small courtyard that leads to my home, which I have turned into a kitchen garden, and there I grow all kinds of herbs and plants that I use solely for magickal purposes. Contrary to popular belief, you really don't need a lot of space for gardening. I have some large raised boxes and tubs dotted around the courtyard, planted with many common herbs, such as parsley, thyme, rosemary, sage, bay, marjoram, and oregano. I also like to grow some of the more unusual, old-fashioned herbs, such as borage, chervil, feverfew, comfrey, sorrel, angelica, lemon balm,

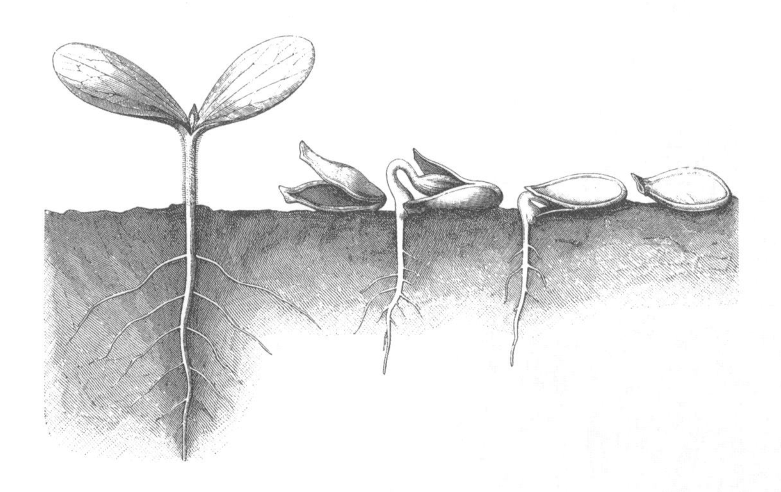

valerian, chamomile, and lovage. I like that you can't easily buy these plants, so you have to sow the seeds and tend to them as they develop. In my opinion, these less-common herbs work much better than the more widely available herbs. They really do make a world of difference to your spellcasting, especially when you blend compatible varieties. Also, not only am I using plants that our ancient ancestors utilized, but I also hope to introduce and encourage up-and-coming witches to embrace these old traditions.

The tending process involves so much more than just planting a seed. You need to connect with a plant by talking to it, touching it each day, complimenting it, and watering it in dry weather. Although I am no expert on the *Farmer's Almanac,* when I am sowing seeds I always feel drawn to the new moon, when gravity pulls water from the earth to the surface. And when I am preparing my oils for anointing, I opt for a full moon, as I consider this phase to be the most magickal time.

This is just my way of doing things, and, in time, I'm sure you will adopt your own ideas.

Why not have a go at growing your own magickal kitchen garden? Once the plants are ready to harvest, pick or cut them, and thank them for their life. Then lay them on trays in a dark room for about a week and, once they are dried, scrunch them up and place them in mason jars. There's something about growing, harvesting, and drying your own herbs that unites the witch and the plant; it amplifies the intent of a spell, making it even more powerful.

## Naturally Magickal Gardens—Deanna

There are some gardens that are just naturally magickal. These are often found residing on ley lines, which are believed by many to be invisible routes of energy that run linearly across the land, connecting old and ancient monuments and places of worship. If there is an old church or ancient religious site within a mile or two from your property, it is possible that your home is either on or near a ley line. The energies they emit are uplifting and healing, often giving you the feeling of elation, happiness, and tranquility. Creatures and wildlife are wholeheartedly attracted to them, and they get a buzz that makes them happy and giddy.

My parents are lucky, as their garden sits directly over a ley line. It's the most tranquil of places that backs onto miles of beautiful English countryside. I have two little Pomeranian dogs, and in the summer we often take them to the garden for a visit. As soon as the dogs arrive, their mood hypes up and they chase around in excited happiness. If I'm ever feeling down or tired, I go to their garden and am instantly uplifted. The energy of the place leaves me feeling recharged and gives me renewed optimism. Strange things happen with the plant life there, too. In the front garden on either side of the driveway, wild garlic has self-seeded and grows in perfect synchronicity. This plant is renowned for its protective properties and you can sense its potent energy when you walk past. Tiny Devon violets carpet another border, encouraging nature spirits and fairy life, and large, strange-looking toadstools tend to pop up overnight.

The other gardens in the street are all pristine and well manicured, but not theirs. Wild red and white heather entwines naturally in another

**border that also houses wild cowslips, celandines, and primroses. At the rear of the house, when in season, tall pink foxgloves stand like sentries, and bluebells grow en masse. Years ago, a rowan tree and a mountain ash self-seeded; these are well known in Britain to give protection against the evil eye and to banish loneliness. When friends come to visit, they feel a sense of peace and remark about the beauty of it all. It's hard to believe that their garden has been mysteriously created but it really has. Some people believe that the spirit world rewards acts of kindness and brings enchantment to their dwellings. My parents are wonderful, generous people, so I'm sure that's the case.**

# MUST-HAVE MAGICKAL GARDEN ORNAMENTS

You can enhance the beauty of your outdoor garden with a few well-placed ornaments. These are not hard to find, and you may see them in yards all over your neighborhood. A witch's garden should be a place of tranquility, meditation, and solitude. There's nothing prettier than having ornamental plates and statues nestled in between flowers or resting proudly on a step. However, few people know the stories and the magickal properties behind them.

- **One of the most common ornaments** to see in a witch's garden is a plaque of the Green Man. He represents protection and is said to keep the animals and vegetation safe and healthy. When creating an herb garden or a vegetable plot, he can be asked to bring abundance and blight-free crops.

- **Salamander ornaments** are a modern trend in garden sculpture, and are usually hung on a fence or placed on a tree. They are purported to have the power of psychic vision and give protection against fire.

- **Unicorn ornaments** tucked into a garden border, or placed under a bush or tree, look truly magical on the night of a full moon. As unicorns know no dark thoughts—only love and purity—they will bring a soothing spiritual ambience to your garden.

- **For those who practice Angelic Wicca,** cherub or angel figurines will balance the mood and bring stillness and blessings.

- **Gazing balls** are reflective orbs that sit in the middle of gardens. They originated in Italy in the thirteenth century, and began to be used in eighteenth-century England as a means of warding off evil spirits. They were made of mirrored glass and filled with string in an attempt to confuse ghosts, demons, and other dark energies. Some people believed that if a dark witch approached the home, she would see herself in the ball's reflection and be scared away. European royalty took an interest in the gazing balls as well, and they were soon seen popping up in regal gardens. Rulers believed that the balls brought prosperity, wealth, security, and wisdom to their property.

- **Moon-gazing hares** are commonplace in a witch's garden, bringing luck and an abundance of magick.

- **Garden gnomes** are often thought of as a kitschy addition to a garden, but they actually have a long history of protecting plants. In the Renaissance era, the Swiss alchemist Paracelsus spoke of gnomes as being nature spirits who appeared at nighttime to help gardens grow. This legend held, and garden gnomes were commonly seen in eighteenth-century yards. Today's gnomes almost always have a red cap and continue to bring health and luster to yards and gardens everywhere!

- **Fairy gardens** made their first appearance in the United States in the late nineteenth century, probably inspired by the displays of tiny bonsai gardens that appeared at the world's fair in Chicago. The miniature worlds represented in these gardens was the subject of a *New York Times* article, which brought the idea to the masses—an idea that morphed into the miniature fairy gardens we see today. The whole idea behind the fairy garden is to give little sprites a safe place to live. In return, they will provide you with good luck. Some things you may want to consider when creating a world for these friends:

  - ★ Include a house of some sort where fairies can rest during the day.
  - ★ Add small plants—things that a person the size of your thumb could tend to.
  - ★ Think about other landscaping items; small rocks can be boulders for your fairies.
  - ★ Add seating or other outdoor resting spots.
  - ★ Consider building your fairy garden in a sheltered area to keep it out of the rain and elements. If you enjoy the elements of this tiny garden, the fairies surely will, too! Scottish folklore tells us that there are two types of fairies: one type is helpful but may play harmless pranks, while the other type is malicious—so if you decide to create a fairy garden, you may want to place little signs that indicate it's for nice fairies only!

# CREATING AN OUTDOOR ANGELIC GARDEN

Angels are universal and are present in many religions. Witches believe that angels have an extremely high spiritual vibration and are here to assist humans throughout their lives. To create an angelic garden, it is best to dedicate a corner of your plot to the angels. You can perform all your outdoor rituals here and grow plants and flowers that resonate with them. An outdoor altar is also lovely if you like to meditate in the garden or if you want to make offerings to your chosen deities.

First, place a small outdoor table or concrete slab on the ground. Obtain a small statue or figurine of an angel and situate this in the center. Resting amethyst and rose quartz crystals nearby will invoke love and peace and balance the energies. If you have soil in the ground you can plant directly into it; if not, plant some of the following flowers in pots, and dot them around your outdoor altar. Following are profiles of some key magickal plants to consider incorporating into your angelic garden. Other plants that are believed to bring magick to the garden are buttercups, carnations, dandelions, lilac, lavender, mistletoe, and roses.

## **Angelica** (*Angelica*)

This plant only attracts positive energy and will sweep away anything negative in its path. It has a connection to the Archangel Michael so its powerful healing properties can help with all kinds of spells for health and well-being. Place angelica root on your altar when casting spells for any kind of healing.

## **Angel's Breath** (*Achillea ptarmica* 'Angel's Breath') **and Baby's Breath** (*Gypsophila*)

The delicate white flowers of baby's plant traditionally adorn brides' bouquets, and are beautiful accompaniments to rose arrangements. Many witches place this flower near a baby at the baby's naming ceremony for good luck. Angel's breath is the flora of romance and family love, so growing it near your outdoor altar will ensure harmony with those you love. If you are looking to attract a partner or soul mate, pick the flowers and entwine them in your hair or dry the flower heads and leave them in a bowl inside your house. Another magickal use for this plant is for help in contacting the spirit world to speak to a loved one who has passed away. Lighting white candles on your altar and asking the angels to open the lines of communication to the spirit world for you can often result in you seeing your loved ones in your dreams.

## **Daffodil** (*Narcissus*)

These gorgeous, goofy blooms are so cheerful that they can change the whole feel of a place. In the fall, plant the bulbs all around your goddess altar and they will hopefully start to bud in time for the spring equinox. As one of the first flowers of spring, daffodils symbolize fertility and growth; they are also wonderful to use in prosperity rituals and can bring luck and good fortune in abundance. Planting other spring flowers alongside daffodils, such as bluebells and crocuses, will make the area look truly enchanting.

## Hollyhocks (*Alcea*)

These impressive flowers have long been associated with the cycle of life and produce eye-catching blooms that are quite spectacular. In folklore, the flower heads were said to be used as skirts for fairies. Try growing wild thyme next to hollyhocks; it is thought to make the fairy world visible to humans. These lovely blooms have a long history in magick. In ancient times, not only were they used for their medicinal properties, but they were also grown to attract abundance and wealth. Today's witches tend to use the dried flower heads in fertility rituals and in potions to bring about success in all things pertaining to work. They are also considered to be the flower of happiness, so they can be used to improve a person's life and bring about happy times.

## Iris (*Iris*)

These striking, showy flowers hold many meanings and there are hundreds of different species. If you receive a piece of jewelry featuring an iris motif or a bouquet containing irises, it is a sign that the giver feels deep sentiment and love for you. Iris is the Greek word for rainbow, and also the name of the Greek goddess of the rainbow; along with Hermes, a messenger of the gods. It is said that purple irises were planted on graves of recently deceased women, so that Iris could guide them on their journey to the underworld. There are numerous iris cultivars with angelic names, including: 'Angel Choir', 'Angel Chiffon', 'Angel Echo', 'Angel Heart', and 'Angel Symphony'.

## Mint (*Mentha*)

To invite angels to your garden, plant mint, as they love the aroma. It's always best to grow any kind of mint in a large pot, as it can spread and take over your garden. There are numerous varieties, but all types are favored by angels and spirit helpers. You can use this plant in rituals to invoke money and luck by placing it on the altar or drying it and carrying it in a pouch when you are out and about. Having mint grow in your angelic garden will ensure that you will never go without the things in life you need.

# MAGICKAL GARDEN FAUNA

To keep nature in balance, many witches are keen to encourage and welcome insects, birds, and other small animals to their gardens. These tiny creatures will grace your outside space with Mother Nature's magick.

## Bring in the Bees

When the right trees and shrubs are planted in a garden, they will bring an abundance of insects for pollination. Bees are especially important for this task because they pollinate flowers, allowing seeds to germinate; without them, humans would struggle to grow food and crops. Worker honeybees only live for several weeks to a few months, depending on the time of year (queens can live three to four years, and drones die after mating), but during that time, they are busy making sure that nature stays in balance. Not only that, but we also have the benefit of their delicious honey, which is full of nutrition and health-giving properties. Many witches love bees and invite them into the garden by planting lots of flowers that bees are attracted to. If you want to attract bees to your garden, try planting any or all of the following: aster, bluebells, butterfly bush, borage (star flower), crocus, honeysuckle, lavatera, lavender, viper's bugloss, and shrubs in the *Mahonia* genus. Some witches even keep their own beehives. If you do keep bees, you will be able to create your own blend of concoctions of honey for healing, eating, and cleansing products, as well as for rituals. You can also make beeswax spell candles, which produce powerful spellcrafting results. Some witches will only use beeswax candles because of their purity.

Following are some of the amazing natural bee by-products that are integral to a witch's holistic health and magickal regimens.

### Bee Propolis

Bee propolis is a brown, resin-like substance that honeybees produce in the hive by mixing their saliva with beeswax and plant matter, such as sap or gum. Propolis is vital to honeybees for their survival. It protects the hive against disease and intrusive parasites, and strengthens the structure of the hive. Its antibacterial properties are well known by healers to fight off sore throats, colds, cold sores, and general aches and pains.

This substance has been in use as far back as 300 BCE and was also used for mummification purposes in ancient Egypt. Propolis is a panacea for most witches, and their natural health-care remedies often include this product in a variety of spells. It represents strength and healing and is believed to contain a great deal of natural power. (*Note*: Avoid propolis if you have asthma, a bleeding disorder, are allergic to bee by-products, or two weeks before a planned surgery.)

## Honey

The taste of honey depends on the type of flower the honeybees derive nectar from, so many apiarists grow specific blossoms to achieve a certain flavor; for instance, lavender for lavender-flavored honey. Wild meadow flower honey is sought after because it is organic and has a lovely floral taste. A productive hive can produce up to 60 pounds (27 kg) of honey a year. Honey can soothe a sore throat, especially when mixed with a few drops of lemon. Also, a teaspoon added to yogurt or hot tea can be refreshing. This ingredient should be in every witch's pantry for cooking, healing, and spellcraft. In Devon, England, where Leanna lives, it is common for monasteries to keep beehives; the honey made is sold to the public to raise funds for the care of their historic buildings. Prince Charles has his own brands of honey from the beehives in his orchards at the Highgrove Estate in Gloucester. The Queen likely has some of it on her breakfast tray to spread on her toast, too!

Honey is an important element in the ceremony of a Wiccan betrothal or handfasting (wedding). The High Priest or High Priestess who conducts this mystical union takes a small silver spoon from the altar and dips it into a crystal receptacle filled with honey. It is then dabbed quickly on the lips of both partners, and they will then be asked to kiss. This will ensure romance and harmony in their relationship.

## Manuka Honey

This special and expensive honey is produced by bees that pollinate the manuka or tea tree (*Leptospermum scoparium*), native to southeast Australia and New Zealand. It has antibacterial components that make it stand out from ordinary honey. It is slightly acidic or tart, and less refined, but still delicious.

Manuka honey is said to be helpful for those who suffer from sore throat, laryngitis, acid reflux, and sinusitis, although studies are ongoing. It is also being studied for mild burn and wound care (although only sterile medical-grade honey is used for this purpose).

## Royal Jelly

Royal jelly is a milky-white nutritive secretion, produced by worker honeybees. All bee larvae are fed royal jelly for the first three days of life, but only the larvae from which a queen will hatch continues to receive royal jelly. The workers are raised with pollen and honey, but the queen continues to dine on royal jelly throughout her life.

Royal jelly comes both jarred and in capsule form, and it is regarded more as a supplement than as a sweetener. Its flavor is totally different from that of honey—it is a bit bitter and sour; fans of fresh royal jelly remark that it is an acquired taste. It can be applied to the skin, but it may cause allergic reactions, so please read the labels carefully, do a patch test before applying liberally, and do your research.

As of yet, it has not been scientifically proven that consuming royal jelly offers health benefits to humans—although some research indicates that it might alleviate symptoms of menopause. It can also be used in rituals to lift your spirits, especially if you've been down in the dumps.

# The Outdoor God and Goddess Garden

**If you favor the Gods and Goddesses, find a little corner of land that you can pledge to your craft and set it up as discussed on page 241 for the angelic garden. Except instead of angel statues and related plants and crystals, incorporate ones that represent and speak to your God(s) or Goddess(es). There are some stunning God and Goddess garden statues available to purchase, and any one of these will look beautiful centered on your slab. You might like to add a small water feature to create the right ambience. Wind chimes and bells are also a nice touch. Add flowers and plants, such as the butterfly bush, to attract butterflies—which are believed to bring hope and blessings to the area—or you could scatter some bluebell seeds, which signify love and gratitude when they are in bloom. Choose a crystal that represents the God or Goddess of your choice and place it directly on the soil. This will amplify the energy around your altar and attract all things good.**

## Never Kill Insects

Most witches deeply care about the planet's ecosystem and, as we look around, we see natural habitats disappearing and being replaced by buildings and parking lots, and countless forms or wildlife suffering and dying from pollution and climate change. Thousands of endangered species face extinction. Those who have a gentle heart feel despair, as there doesn't seem to be a lot that can be done about it. There are over 1.1 million different species of insects on our planet, and only around one to three percent of them are considered pests. Insects are vital to the earth's health, so we must try to protect them. By planting lots of flowers and trees, you can encourage their survival. In addition to the bee- and butterfly-friendly plants mentioned on pages 245 and 248, think about planting some of these: angelica, black-eyed Susan, cosmos, dill, cornflower, mountain mint, and tickseed.

## Visiting Felines

Cats are psychic and are attracted to the craft or those who practice anything magickal. Quite often, sick, lost, or hungry cats will visit a witch's garden to find some peace and solace. Planting catmint for them is akin to a gin and tonic and relaxes their mood, bringing them joy and peace. Stray cats know who they want to be with, and strong bonds can often blossom when one regularly visits the garden. Please be patient when neighbors' cats saunter in. Yes, they dig up your onions and poop in your borders, but it's likely your garden is special and that's why they are attracted to it. As much as most witches adore feline energy—many keep a cat or two as a familiar—cats unfortunately do not mix well with birds, and are a major avian predator. Consider putting a bell on your cat's collar to warn birds that your pet is in the yard, and hang any bird feeders in a place where cats can't jump up and reach them.

## GARDENING BY THE MOON

For thousands of years, people have been growing herbs and plants according to the lunar phases. The great success of these gardeners is due to a couple of factors, including the moon's gravitational pull and its light—both of which affect the growth of the entire plant, from roots to leaves.

Here is how to use the moon's phases to your planting advantage:

- **During the new moon,** tides are at their highest, as the moon has its strongest gravitational pull on the earth during this time. Groundwater is also affected by the lunar pull during this phase, making it the perfect time to plant. Seeds and roots gain instant access to groundwater, giving the plants an instant growth boost.
- **While the moon is waxing** (leading up to the full moon), plant leaves are exposed to plenty of light, even in the nighttime hours, which allows for added growth.
- **When the moon is full,** the gravitational pull of the moon on the earth's water is amplified again, which gives the roots another chance to use groundwater to their advantage.
- **As the full moon fades,** that gravitational pull lets up. The roots and leaves of the plant get a little rest at this time and their growth slows.
- **When the new moon begins,** the entire cycle repeats itself.

Take a look at your calendar and mark the start of the next lunar phase. And please take note—you don't have to plant in the dark! The energy of the current moon phase is active whether it's noon or midnight.

A lovely ritual to do on the first night of a changing moon, whether it is visible or not, is to take a few minutes to stare up at the sky and connect to the moon's power. Some witches like to go outside and sit on the ground for a while (weather permitting) so they can connect with the earth at the same time. By placing one hand on the ground, and the other stretched above, you can feel at one with the Universe. Many witches will chant a few lines in their own words, giving thanks to their chosen deity.

# Chapter 10

# Mystical Trees and Magickal Wands

TREES ARE VITAL TO THE PLANET BECAUSE THEY ARE the lungs of the earth—they purify our air by absorbing carbon dioxide and releasing oxygen—and are home to a variety of wildlife as well. Trees are also crucial to witches. We like to wrap our arms around tree trunks to feel their vibrational energy or sit quietly beneath them. (When the weather is fine, Shawn often ventures out and sits underneath a tree. Find a really old one with large, winding roots and place your hands on the ground; you can feel the vibrational energy buzzing underneath your fingertips.) And, we also incorporate trees into our spellcraft in many ways. The leaves and small twigs can be collected and used as altar items, and the larger twigs and branches can be made into wands. (*Note*: Try to use fallen leaves, twigs, or branches, if possible, and be sure to always thank the tree for its gifts!)

Wands have been used in magick throughout the centuries, and these magickal power rods are created as conductors to make a witch's spell extra potent. As with any kind of plant, each type of tree possesses its own magickal properties. Over time, a witch will accumulate a variety of wands, all made from different types of wood. They are used to cast a circle at the beginning of a ritual and to draw down power from the moon. They can also be present on the altar during any spellcasting or kept beside you when you need a particular energy the wood might emit.

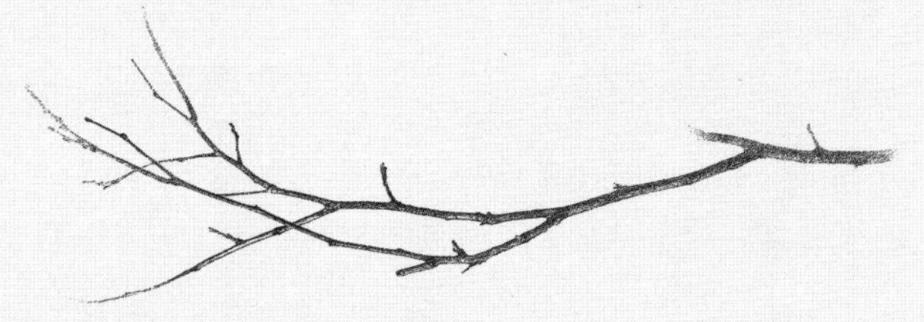

## FOUR KEY MAGICKAL TREES

A number of trees are considered to be magickal; the following four are among the most powerful. If you have room for a tree on your land, think about planting one if it is native to your area; if not, go to a park or woodland and pick out a favorite. You can return to the same spot again and again, and try to form a relationship with it. Remember that all trees are alive, they each have their own soul and their own personality, and many have nature spirits residing by their roots.

## Apple Tree (*Malus domestica*)

The apple has gotten a bad rap ever since its starring role in the story of Adam and Eve. Yes, it's been saddled with an unfortunate reputation, but at its core (no pun intended), the apple tree's energy encourages us to ask what we have denied ourselves. What kind of pleasures in life have we said no to, thinking them too dangerous or outside our comfort zone?

To be sure, limits are a good thing. They keep us from hurting ourselves and other people. However, sometimes we impose restrictions on our lives for no reason other than a belief that we can't achieve certain goals. Maybe you'd love to see the view from a mountaintop, but think you think you aren't capable of making the climb—even though you've never tried. Perhaps you are thinking about leaving your job for a new career that feels like a calling, but you're afraid of what people might say or that you might fail. Maybe you just want to try a wild new haircut, but you wonder how your loved ones will react!

Most of us have some simple heartfelt desires that we are perfectly capable of realizing but haven't. Apples encourage us to think about those aspirations and decide once and for all—will we be courageous in our ambition or will we set those old longings aside for good?

### Apple Tree and Magick

- **Use an apple on your altar as a tool to attract love.** Place the apple on a cutting board, on its side (stem facing to the right or left). Cut the apple in half, and you will see the shape of a pentacle. Place each half on the altar when you are casting spells for love and the apple will bring a wealth of magick to your spell.
- **Include apple seeds in spells for protection,** as they are renowned for having protective properties. Place a few apple seeds inside poppets or pouches to give the magick more power.
- **Apples make perfect decorations for Samhain,** as they represent abundance, protection, love, and happiness so try drying some apple slices and create an autumn wreath, along with some seasonal flowers. Hang the wreath on the front door to invite abundance to your dwelling.
- **Summon what you need.** At Samhain, cut an apple in half as noted above. To bring about good fortune, eat one half and bury the other and you will attract exactly what you need from life.

## Hawthorn (*Crataegus*)

This thorny-branched genus of small trees or shrubs is a highly regarded tree in witchcraft. The tree produces white, pink, or red flowers and red berries that have long been used to treat heart and circulatory issues. (*Note*: Never self-treat yourself with hawthorn; it can have many side effects and interact with various medications. Be sure to discuss this with your doctor beforehand.)

Hawthorn is also a source of myth and mystery. According to Irish folklore, it is one of several trees (or shrubs) that can induce sleep and open a portal to the fairy world. In "The Fairy Thorn," an old ballad by Sir Samuel Ferguson, a group of young women sneak away from their chores to dance and sing in the forest. Alas, they fall into a trance-like state underneath a hawthorn tree, and three of the girls watch helplessly as their friend Anna Grace is taken away by fairies, never to be seen again!

Hawthorn is the fairy tree, and legend has it that harming a hawthorn will bring the wrath of the fairies down on the perpetrator.

## Hawthorn and Magick

- **Making love underneath the hawthorn** is believed to promote fertility. If you are not so brave as to get busy in public, you can place a few leaves from the tree somewhere near your bedside.
- **Cast love spells by writing the traits** of your ideal mate on a piece of paper and burying it under a hawthorn tree.
- **Prevent negative energies from entering your home** by planting the tree somewhere near the front of your house.
- **Protect babies in their cradles from evil spirits** by drying hawthorn blossoms and leaving them in a bowl by the crib (but out of reach of the baby!).
- **Create a powerful wand from a hawthorn branch** that sanctifies your altar.
- **Place some stones or crystals in a circle** under the tree for the fae folk.

## **Indian Sandalwood** (*Santalum album*)

Sandalwood is one of the most valuable trees on the planet. The oil distilled from the trees has a familiar, woodsy scent, one that is used in everything from perfumes and colognes to air fresheners. It is a very slow-growing tree that can take fifty to eighty years to reach full maturity. The downside of this leisurely growth means that younger trees are overharvested and it has become endangered. In its native regions of Southeast Asia, sandalwood is harvested for wood chips, powder, and essential oil. Nag Champa, which is probably the most popular incense, is a combination of sandalwood and various floral scents; it's used in magick and spellcraft throughout the world. In India, sandalwood is also made into intricate carvings, placed on sacred funeral pyres, and used as an anointing paste in Hindu rituals.

Traditional Chinese medicine and Ayurvedic medicine have used sandalwood for hundreds of years to treat digestive disorders, liver problems, respiratory issues, urinary tract infections, and skin eruptions. More recent health findings indicate that sandalwood may help to calm anxiety, increase awareness and alertness, promote wound healing by increasing cell growth and turnover, and it may even help to kill skin cancer cells. (*Note*: As ongoing research continues, as always, consult your health-care provider before embarking on any regimen incorporating sandalwood.)

## Sandalwood and Magick

- **As incense, sandalwood protects** against evil spirits and is used in exorcism rituals.
- **If you mix sandalwood with lavender,** it can conjure protective and helpful spirits.
- **Burn sandalwood incense or sprinkle** sandalwood powder around the outside of your house for protection.
- **Burn a piece of sandalwood** to promote psychic visions or clarity of mind during meditation.
- **Sandalwood can help you** get the things you desire most by writing your wish on a piece of bark.

# Willow (*Salix*)

The willow is such a graceful tree, as it bows and bends to the forces of nature through the years. The willow tree pulls water from its surroundings with its deep roots—and, of course, these roots allow it to adapt to almost any kind of weather without being overwhelmed.

Willow shows us how to handle emotional storms while maintaining our poise and dignity. This tree encourages us to be fluid, to go with the flow, and reminds us that even after a barrage of hard times, we will remain standing tall and proud.

If you have a willow in your yard or in a park, stand underneath it. Watch as it moves back and forth in the

wind without putting up much resistance. This is not to say that you should let people walk all over you—but don't allow your emotions to get the better of you. Think of the way the willow moves as a slow inhalation and exhalation of energy. Envision this the next time you find yourself battling anger or rage. Like the willow, you can learn to shift the energy in the next moment and let it go.

### Willow and Magick

- **Calm your emotions with willow;** if you ever get angry or overly anxious, the magick from a willow leaf will have a calming effect.
- **Single people looking to attract new love** might want to carry a small amount of willow bark in their bag or on their person.
- **Protect yourself from evil and nightmares;** both the leaves and the bark of a willow tree offer protection from evil and psychic attack. Sleep with a small willow branch under your bed or dry some leaves and place them in a bowl on your night table. Your dreams will be sweet and you'll be protected all night long.
- **Connect with your inner self.** The enchanting willow unleashes your inspiration and helps you get in touch with your feminine side. Place any part of the tree on your altar when spellcasting.

## HOW TO MAKE YOUR OWN WAND

Wand-making is such a peaceful exercise and it's really good for the soul. Because of this, it is not uncommon for many witches to make extra wands and sell their creations online. When you buy one from a reputable seller, you can pretty much be assured that they hold positive energy, but if you want to connect with your wand on a more spiritual level, there is no better way than to whittle your own. The best wands are often crafted from a twig or a small branch that has fallen from a tree. The bark is carefully stripped off and then rubbed with sandpaper to make it smooth. Your wand can be painted, varnished, and decorated (see opposite page).

Take a stroll in the woods or a park, somewhere nearby, that has an array of different trees. While you are walking around, take special note of how you are feeling and venture toward the trees that call out to you. Whenever I (Leanna) am in pursuit of a new wand, I place my hands on the trunk of the tree to see if I can feel any energy emanating from it. Sometimes, I might get a tingly feeling, or I might sense an instant connection to it. You need to touch and inspect the branches; it may sound strange, but try talking to the tree telepathically. You also might see a large twig on the ground that you are drawn to. If this is the case, pick it up and examine it. Although, traditionally, a wand should measure from the elbow to the tip of your middle finger—around 13 inches (33 cm)—I've always found that the size doesn't really matter. As long as you feel some kind of bond with the tree, that is what counts.

Once you have decided on a twig, the most important thing to do is silently ask the tree if you can take it. It's never good manners to just gather up what you want and head off home; you must respect the fact that the tree is a living thing. If you feel the tree saying yes, then thank it for its offering.

## Whittle It!

Here are the steps for making your own wand:

1. **CARVE IT:** Take a sharp knife and carefully carve off the bark to expose the wood underneath (this may take a while).

2. **SAND IT:** Use sandpaper to rub the wand until it is completely smooth (this may also take a while).

3. **VARNISH OR PAINT IT:** You can use a clear varnish if you want to keep it looking natural or you might opt to paint it with a tinted varnish or semi-gloss paint. If you are making your wand for a particular purpose, choose a color that will best influence your spell:

    - **BLUE:** For spells involving family and friendships
    - **GREEN:** For spells involving money and wealth
    - **YELLOW:** For spells involving health and well-being
    - **PINK:** For spells involving love, marriage, and relationships
    - **RED:** For spells involving work and business
    - **PURPLE:** For spells involving spiritual matters

4. **DECORATE IT:** This is your wand, so you can decorate it any way you see fit. You can glue crystals or glitter on it, wrap it in silver or gold wire, affix feathers to it, tie it with ribbons—use your imagination.

5. **BLESS AND EMPOWER IT:** When your wand is finished, it's important to bless and empower it. In the evening, venture outdoors and hold your wand in both hands. Say this mantra three times:

*"I summon the energies of the cosmos*
*to bring magick to this vessel.*

*Enable its power this night, under the luna light."*

After you have spoken the words, carefully place your wand on the ground (or if you're in an apartment, on a moonlit windowsill) and leave it overnight to soak up the moon's rays.

The more you work your wand into spellcraft, the more powerful it will become, so start using it right away.

## Casting a Circle before a Spell

Whatever spell you are casting, when all your items are positioned on your altar, take the wand in your right hand and wave it clockwise in a circle over the objects. This practice creates a protective force field, allowing nothing outside the circle to contaminate your spell. When the spell is complete, you can either put your wand to bed by wrapping it in a pretty colored cloth or, if you would rather have it on display, find a special spot in your home where it will live. Leanna has a beautiful glass cabinet her husband made for her where all her wands are displayed.

# The Craft of Wand-Making—Leanna

I started making wands when I first took an interest in Wicca as a young woman, and there's nothing more satisfying than holding your finished creation. I always like to sleep with a new wand next to my bed for a few weeks—but I'm a bit of a "wandaholic" and have lots of them in my collection.

It is strange, but during the process of making a wand, I get a real sense of being at one with nature, and, afterward, my body actually feels like it is filled with powerful magick. I also experience vivid dreams in the nights that follow, so I'm sure there's so much more that happens to your soul when you set about making one. The one thing I know for certain is that your cherished item will serve you and your craft for a lifetime, so get outdoors, walk that woodland, and find yourself a new best friend.

## DIFFERENT KINDS OF WAND WOOD

With so many varieties of trees in the world, you would have to be an expert to simply look at one and know which type it was. Thankfully, we have it much easier today. There are a number of apps that you can download to your phone where you can photograph a tree and the app will instantly identify the species. You can then do your research and find out the properties of the wood and incorporate it into your magic.

### Alder (*Alnus*)

Used primarily to represent the elements in altar magick, an alder wand is perfect if you want to cast spells for protection, to enhance your psychic abilities, or to draw in prosperity if you're having money problems. Whenever Leanna does readings, she always has her alder wand nearby, as it helps her tune into the person and their life.

### Apple Tree (*Malus domestica*)

Apple is a powerful wood with so many properties. It won't work for everyone because it has an extremely high vibration, which means it takes time—months or even a year sometimes—to connect with its owner. You might have to be patient. Once you do form a connection with it, use it for fertility rituals, divination, and anything having to do with love and affairs of the heart.

## **Ash** (*Fraxinus*)

An ash wand is very loyal to its owner, so it's best not to hand it down to others in the family, as it might refuse to work. This is a powerful healer and can be used alongside Reiki or other healing practices. Although it does have other properties, keep the ash wand solely for when you need to perform any kind of healing ritual (emotional or physical).

## **Beech** (*Fagus*)

Many consider beechwood to have artistic energy, so it suits those who are into art, sculpture, or anything creative. Because a beech branch makes a beautiful-looking wand, it will bring happiness and joy to its owner. Use it in spells to boost your creativity and open up your imagination. Leanna keeps one by her computer when she is writing, as it helps to inspire her.

## **Birch** (*Betula*)

European witches tend to use wands made of birch—sometimes called the "Lady of the Woods"—to remove evil spirits, but it's generally thought to help with calming emotions and cleansing the area where it sits. When a witch is sad, she will use this to clear away any negativity, inviting new ways of thinking. Even having one of these wands in the home works as a daily cleanser, leaving the property free of any bad vibes.

## **Cedar** (*Cedrus*)

This wand invokes money and wealth and is best suited to any rituals where you need to boost your finances. It's also used in spells to improve businesses and earnings and works especially well if there's a pot of basil nearby. Use it whenever you need to cast a love spell for someone or for protection from the evil eye.

## **Chestnut** (*Castanea*)

This wand is multipurpose and excellent in rituals for healing and calming down emotions. It releases a calming effect and is very good at soothing upsets in the home. For some reason, it works exceptionally well with psychic male witches who like to astrally travel and predict future events.

## **Dogwood** (*Cornus*)

Not only is this wood beautiful to look at, with its vibrant colors of red, but it can also produce enchanting magick for optimism and well-being. This wand likes instruction, so it is best used in any verbal spells for removing depression, lifting a person's spirits, and casting out negative emotions.

## **Elder** (*Sambucus*)

There have been many witches, even accomplished ones, who have struggled with this wand. It can sometimes be unresponsive and take a long time to connect with its owner. If you are lucky enough to have one work for you, cast spells to bring in happiness and contentment, remove worries and concerns, or for any exorcisms or hauntings, and then let us know your secret, as Leanna's has been dormant for years!

## Elm (*Ulmus*)

If you are proficient in your magickal practices, this wand will suit you. It needs a confident owner who really knows their craft, and only then will it serve you well. In spellcasting, it is brilliant for alleviating loneliness or enticing new friends into your life. Oftentimes, elm wands are made much smaller than usual, which is handy because you can carry them around in your purse to give you an extra confidence boost.

## Fir (*Abies*)

This one responds well to steady, reliable people. If you are a "head in the clouds" type, it might not be the wand for you, as it works best for people who have strong leadership qualities. It is popular with male witches who might wish to remedy the ills of the world. I have a wonderful friend who keeps this wand purely for the purpose of spellcasting for the animal kingdom and to dispel suffering for the animals.

## **Hawthorn** (*Crataegus*)

Associated with fairies and nature spirits, this wand is best used when casting spells outdoors or to protect the animal kingdom in general. Leanna likes to use this whenever she needs to do a spell for one of her pets. Whether your pet is having a behavioral issue or they are sick (bring them to the vet, too, in this case), this very powerful wand never fails.

## **Hazel** (*Corylus*)

A very sensitive wand that will be devoted to its owner, a hazel wand often refuses to work for anyone else, so a witch is likely to be buried with it upon death. This wand may also be used as a water dowser and is said to emit an ethereal mist over unfound water sources. It works particularly well in spells involving real estate or if a house move is blocked, and, like the alder wand, it supports a psychic witch if placed on the table during a reading.

## **Ivy** (*Hedera*)

Although ivy is not really a tree or a bush (it's actually a woody vine), some species have thick, woody, twig-like stems. Ivy wands are mystical and magickal and work well for female witches, as they are associated with the feminine. They can be used in love magic or for healing broken relationships, as well as in rituals where someone might need to summon inner strength. It has protective qualities and is a great healer. This is probably one of Leanna's favorite wands of all because it's so versatile, and it brings added oomph to any spell.

## Larch (*Larix*)

Larch wands are good for giving a confidence boost and are used in spells when people might be taking exams or going on job interviews. It opens the channels of communication and boosts low self-esteem. Some witches also use this wand to make a connection with their muse, especially if they are working on a creative project.

## Lilac (*Syringa vulgaris*)

This wood is ruled by Venus and is a go-to wand for any love spells you might wish to perform. It works particularly well to bring about harmony during and after a divorce or for helping a person move on after a relationship is over. It has a knack for calming down frayed nerves and soothing tempers, enabling a person to see things clearly. Its other properties include clearing hauntings and banishing unwanted spirits.

## Maple (*Acer*)

This is a very lively wand, which prefers its owner to be out and about in the world. It will respond to different climates, adventures, and challenges. So, if you are a quiet, stay-at-home type, this wand might not be suitable for you. Use it to cast spells for new beginnings, clearing away old problems, and embarking on a different path.

## **Oak** (*Quercus*)

This is a must-have wand for all witches. It's traditional, it's powerful, and it will help you out when times are hard. If you are dealing with any problematic situation in your life, meditating with an oak wand will allow you to draw in strength and will steer you through the many obstacles up ahead. Use it in spells to clear away stumbling blocks and in spells to help bring about strength when needed.

## **Poplar** (*Populus*)

Poplar has very moralistic energy and will only work with a person who has the highest integrity and vision. A witch will benefit from this when they want to attract wisdom or to reveal any hidden secrets. It also works well if you have lost something and can't find it. Just carry the wand around with you and ask it to direct you. Use it on Saturdays when you want to cast spells for protection and safety. Leanna made a few tiny ones for her kids when they were little to carry in their bags when they were away from home.

## **Rowan or Mountain Ash** (*Sorbus*)

This is probably the most powerful wand of all and one we would advise every witch to make. It has amazing protective qualities, creating a shield against any kind of evil or anything untoward. It also possesses healing properties, so it is good for using in magick when someone is unwell, and it draws in success and promotes psychic abilities. It is particularly good for spellcasting against unruly neighbors, violent partners, burglars, and unscrupulous merchants.

## **Willow** (*Salix*)

Willow is sacred to the moon and the Goddess, so it's wonderful for any kind of lunar magick or spells that are cast under the moon. This is the essential wand to use when someone has experienced hardship or illness, and it can turn a bad experience into a positive one. It also boosts strength and endurance, it is all healing, and it settles down unhappy thoughts.

## **Yew** (*Taxus*)

Tradition has it that yew wands should be crafted from the roots of the tree, rather than the branches, and are collected when a tree blows down in a storm. They are usually twisted and gnarly and incredibly pretty but, in the past, they were used by warlocks who practiced black magick. It's not a wand Leanna has in her collection, but today, it is more commonly utilized to protect against the dark arts, which could be why so many yew trees are found in graveyards in England. If you think you've been cursed or you have experienced a barrage of bad luck, use this wand to repel any dark energies.

Chapter 11

# Magickal Animals

**FOR CENTURIES, ANIMALS AND WITCHES HAVE SHARED** a close bond—especially cats, as they are psychic and are attracted to those who practice anything magickal. Although not every witch is an animal devotee, most of us have a deep affinity with them. A true witch will endeavor to have at least one animal as a companion, or familiar, in their lifetime. Many of today's witches believe that each creature has a soul, from the tiniest insect to the most massive beasts. Within each species, every individual has its own unique personality, just as humans do, with their own mannerisms, quirks, and behaviors. This becomes even more apparent if you have ever owned more than one dog or cat.

Witches also believe in the creed "harm none," which encompasses all the creatures living on earth. Some practice the creed by becoming vegetarian or vegan, whereas others practice it more broadly, making sure that they would never intentionally hurt or harm another living being. Our animals don't have a voice, so we need to try our best to treat them with respect and love; in return, they will reward us with their loyalty.

Even creatures that we fear have souls, and have a right to be appreciated. So if, for instance, you see a huge black spider in the bathtub, don't wash it down the drain—find a way to carefully scoop it up and release it outside. While we are on the subject of spiders, witches believe that spiders are one of the very few animals on earth that fully understand the human language. Often, if we politely ask them to leave, it's not uncommon for them to comply by scampering away. Imagine how frightening it must be if you're a tiny spider and you see some great big giant of a person trying to bash you with a huge slipper. Try to put yourself in their situation, and, if the roles were reversed, envision how that would make you feel. They might look scary, but they can't help that.

Any insect, be it a moth, an ant, or a tiny beetle, has a right to be here. Sometimes, when infestations occur, we must rethink our methods because it's just not practical to share the same space. If you ever find yourself in this situation, just try to deal with things as humanely as possible. It's sad, and there are many witches worldwide who struggle with this.

## TUNE INTO THE ANIMAL WORLD

It's so good for our soul to interact and intermingle with the animal kingdom. If you're fortunate enough to have a garden, start feeding the birds. You can purchase a small bird table or feeder, and buy some nuts to hang in trees (only use unseasoned nuts—raw nuts are best—and hang them in a special bird nut feeder to deter squirrels). Even those without a garden can place smaller feeders on windowsills. Once your feathered friends start to visit you, they will come back year after year until you have fed many generations of birdlife. You might also like to attract hedgehogs, which are considered among British witches to be very lucky to have in the garden.

Another way to bond with animal vibration is to visit woodlands or forests. Heading outdoors into nature is a great way to tune into the animal vibration. Sit quietly under a tree somewhere and place your hands on the ground. Beneath your fingers will be an array of wildlife—tiny insects all curious about the energy you release. Listen to the birdsong and send the birds a loving message in your mind. Every thought is a living thing, and although there is no scientific proof as yet, witches believe that animals communicate on some kind of telepathic level, so if you send them good energy, they will receive it.

## OUR TREASURED PETS

If you've ever visited an animal shelter or a (reputable) breeder to seek out a new animal companion, there is usually one dog or cat that you are immediately drawn to. This happens quite naturally when you psychically tune into the energy and vibration of the animal. During this time, we must trust our instincts and listen to our inner truth. Once we have made a choice, we then go on to form fierce bonds with our pets: they become our children, and over time we love them so much, our hearts could literally burst.

## Finding the Right Pet for You

Not every witch can psychically tune into animals, so if you want to make sure you are choosing the right pet for you, you can do this small ritual beforehand. Fluorite is probably the best crystal to use because it clears away mental clutter, leaving your mind clear to focus on the task at hand.

### MATERIALS

- A small piece of fluorite
- A piece of paper and a pen
- A lighter
- A fireproof bowl
- A drawstring bag

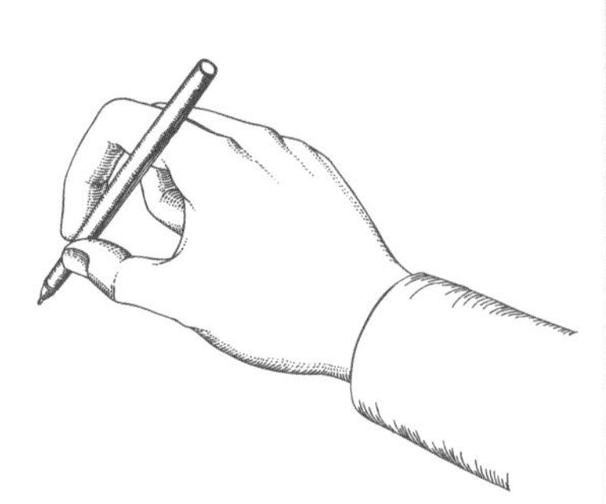

### RITUAL

On the piece of paper, write down the following incantation:

*"I am light, I am free,*
*I clear my mind so I can see*
*The right familiar, come to me,*
*With love and blessings, so mote it be."*

Holding the crystal in your hand, take the other items and venture outdoors. It doesn't matter where you go, just try to find a place where you can be alone for a few minutes. Say the incantation three times and then place the paper in the bowl and set it on fire. Watch the ashes and smoke rise upward. Your message has now been sent to the Universe.

Once the remaining ashes have cooled, place them in the drawstring bag, along with the piece of fluorite, and take the bag with you to the shelter or breeder. Once you arrive at your destination, sprinkle the ashes on the ground outside and hold the crystal in your hand the whole time.

Pay attention to how you feel when you meet the animals for the first time. Spend as much time as you can with each one and, if you're allowed to, pet and stroke them. There might be one or two that you instinctively know are not right for you and that's okay. To help them find the right home, send a positive thought to the animal and make a wish for them to find the perfect human companions. This is a very important time in your life because you are seeking out a new family member. Don't rush anything and keep digging deep within yourself for a sign that you have found the right one. Witches believe that everything happens for a reason, so it's safe to say that while you are making this important choice, your spirit helper will most definitely be by your side, guiding you in the right direction.

## Connect with Your Pet

Because pets' lives are much shorter than ours, many witches tend to lavish attention on their fur-babies, giving them copious amounts of love and devotion. Witches also like to sit quietly with their pets and practice the art of telepathic communication. This can be really handy, especially if you have acquired your furry friend from a shelter. They may have a bad habit you'd like to correct, or you might want to help them dispel any fears they might have.

Whatever breed of pet you have, this ritual will enable you to make a connection.

## RITUAL

To begin, either sit with your pet on your lap or sit beside them. Make sure you are relaxed and that there are no distractions. You might want to play some soothing music, too, to create the right ambience.

Close your eyes and place a hand gently on their back. If your pet is shy about being touched, just hover your hand over their back. Clear your mind and imagine that you are both inside a large golden bubble. In your mind, ask your guide to stay close by and send loving, healing rays through your hand to your pet. You will know when it's working because your pet may relax or even shiver a little.

Telepathically, tell your pet how much you love them and that you will always be there for them. Ask them to trust you.

If you have anything in particular that you'd like to say to them, now is the time. If they're nervous, inform them that you will never let anything hurt them; or if they are excitable all the time, ask them to remain calm. If they're not yet house-trained, you might even ask them to do their business outside instead of on the carpet.

If you establish a connection with your pet, it is possible that you might suddenly have a random thought or message pop into your head. During this bonding, pay attention to everything that enters your mind, as your pet might be trying to communicate with you! They could be saying that they'd like more exercise, or they don't like the children shouting. Don't dismiss these feelings; simply reply by saying you will do your best to change things.

Stay in your golden bubble for as long as you can or until your pet has had enough and wanders off.

Over time, this form of magickal communication really does work. You may have to repeat the exercise daily for a few months until your animal companion recognizes and accepts you as part of their life. Animals are especially responsive to crystals, so some witches will perform this exercise with a piece of amethyst nearby. If you want to know more about this, you can find out about all the different types of crystals to use for your pets in one of our other books, *The Crystal Witch*.

I'm sure that many of you with fur-babies already do this, but for those who don't, it's important to communicate with your pet verbally, too. Dogs and cats especially, love it when you talk to them. Always say good morning, never stop telling them how much you love them, and always give them a kiss goodnight. Pet them and cuddle them as much as possible. (Stroking an animal's fur and hearing it breathe or purr will soothe and cleanse any tension you might be feeling, too.) You have to pack a lifetime of love into the short years they have on this planet.

## ANIMAL GRIEF—HEALING BROKEN HEARTS

As this book is all about witchy well-being, we thought it might be right to cover the emotional connections we have with our animals. Many witches develop lovely, long-lasting relationships with our pets, which bring so much joy and comfort to us throughout our lives. Of course, however much happiness they bring, the pain of them growing old and passing away can be truly devastating.

If your pet has left this earth, you will undoubtedly be suffering from grief. It can be pretty overwhelming and traumatic, and we may not get the same level of comfort from people around us as we might get if a human member of our family passed away. Most witches are firm believers that when it is your time to pass, you will see your cherished pets again. We know that there is a special place in the spirit world that is created purely for the animal kingdom. Many know it as the Rainbow Bridge, a supposed celestial meadow with glorious scenery where your pet will reside until they are reunited with you upon your death. If you have read *The Witch's Way*, another book we wrote together, there is a more detailed description of how we came to know about the Rainbow Bridge and its significance. It is a comforting thought, knowing that there is a place in the spirit world assigned just to pets. Many avid animal lovers on earth who pass over into the spirit world will act as caregivers for our pets until we return to them. Time passes much more quickly for our deceased pets, and, apparently, they get very excited at the prospect of seeing us again. Until then, they might visit you from their astral plane and insert themselves into your dreams. It's also not uncommon for them to make

their presence known vocally. Many people have heard a familiar bark or meow after their pet has passed, and some even felt a heaviness on the bed where their pet used to sleep.

It's natural to grieve for a lost pet, so just ignore anyone who says, "Oh, it's just a cat, for goodness sake" or "It's only a dog; pull yourself together!" This little soul was part of your family, and you have every right to feel the way you do; it is altogether natural to love and miss them. However, if your grief is prolonged and you just can't get over it, there are magickal ways to ease the pain. These kinds of spells don't eradicate your emotions, but they do leave you feeling at peace with it all and will help you to think and talk about your pet without falling apart. These rituals can help you control your emotions and assist you in being more accepting of their passing.

## Animal Ashes

Whether you have chosen to bury your pet or have them cremated, many witches purchase or make little headstones or plaques for their deceased pets. They are often engraved with the pet's name and perhaps show a photograph. If you have a garden, find a nice little spot for your pet. You can plant a small shrub or some flowering bulbs in a pot and situate it nearby the site.

If you don't have a garden, you might consider an animal cemetery—beautiful places that are sensitively created to keep memories alive for the owners and the children of the families who have had pet losses. When you visit your pet's final resting place, lay some crystals on the ground where the ashes are scattered or where you have them buried. Uplifting crystals to use include chrysoprase, malachite, rhodochrosite, and rose quartz (see page 284).

You could also visit the beach to source driftwood, shells, or large pebbles that you can paint with the pentagram symbol to protect your departed animal. Or, cut out a picture of your pet and paste it onto a large flat pebble. To ensure that it doesn't fade, brush yacht varnish over it to keep it pristine, and then rest it on top of the soil. You can then scatter the ashes of your pet around it.

The only thing we wouldn't recommend is to keep your pet's ashes in the house for a long time. If you can, scatter them around their final resting place. This might be the garden where they played or a field where you used to walk them. Remember, they are in the most fantastic place, with no restrictions or boundaries. Set the ashes free and rejoice in their passing.

## Saying Farewell

Ceremonies and rituals have a knack for making you feel better, especially when there is nothing practical left to do.

Stand in front of your familiar's grave and give a photo of your pet to each family member present. Hold the picture over your heart, and ask each person to sprinkle some salt (for purification) over the ground where the ashes are to be scattered. Say the following mantra once:

***"My saddened heart I'm sure will mend,***
***As your spirit flies into the sky,***
***Blessed be my treasured friend;***
***I kiss you as I wave goodbye."***

Then, kiss the photograph. Afterward, frame each of the pictures and place them around the house. Make sure you tend to the area regularly and keep it looking pretty.

## Easing the Grief

Here is another ritual you can do to help with the heartache of losing a familiar. The mixture of herbs and oil has a lovely calming effect and, when mixed together, can lift your mood.

### MATERIALS

1 teaspoon dried lavender

1 teaspoon dried coriander

1 teaspoon dried chamomile

1 teaspoon dried basil

7 drops rose essential oil

A small purple or white gauze drawstring bag

### RITUAL

In a bowl, blend all of the herbs and sprinkle in the rose essential oil.

When they are mixed well, transfer them to a small purple or white gauze drawstring bag. Keep the pouch somewhere on your person for a week, in a pocket or pinned to your garments. At night place it under your pillow. As you sleep, these herbs will help to heal the sadness and heartbreak you're feeling. In about a week, you should start to feel much better, so then you can distribute the mixture all around your pet's memorial.

## The Four Important Heart-Healing Crystals

These four key crystals are instrumental in helping you heal after a loss, in your own time.

**CHRYSOPRASE:** This powerful apple-green crystal can lift melancholy, especially long-term sadness and grief. When placed next to herbs like basil, lavender, and sage, it can act as a great magnifier to soothe emotional wounds and heal the heart of mourning. If there is a question mark about the cause of death, divine truth will eventually reveal the cause.

**MALACHITE:** This stone is often worn by grieving witches in the form of jewelry. You can find some lovely pieces online: earrings, necklaces, and bracelets that work beautifully. Malachite acts as a grounding stone, bringing acceptance and invoking strength.

**RHODOCHROSITE:** This beautiful pink crystal evokes compassion and forgiveness for oneself and helps to strip away blame, healing any broken hearts in its path.

**ROSE QUARTZ:** When a person is grieving or is grappling with a terrible sadness, the heart chakras can pop out of alignment. This crystal's vibration is finely tuned to the individual and, if carried or worn, will lessen the pain of loss.

# THE COLLECTIVE CONSCIOUSNESS

This isn't a pleasant subject to write about, but we both think that it's necessary. Many witches are animal rights activists and do everything they can to try to protect not just kept animals but wildlife and natural habitats. Every time you turn on social media or open a newspaper, you'll read reports or accounts of animal cruelty. Many witches are super sensitive, and this kind of media coverage leaves an aching inside their hearts. Although there are numerous solitary witches worldwide, it's an excellent idea to write a blog or join a Wiccan group online and ask like-minded folk to cast a spell with you at a specific time. When you have multiple witches all saying the same incantation at the same time, it can cause a shift of energy that might make a difference.

Some years ago, I (Leanna) formed a coven, and once a month, on a full moon, my witch friends and I would meet up and combine our magic. We would often conduct rituals to help the animals of the world, to protect them from abuse. I find it tremendously powerful to engage in collective magic. Although it's great to all get together, you don't necessarily have to be physically standing next to another person to make this work. What produces the power is the thoughts and the intent of the spell being projected to the universe.

## A Spell to Stop Animal Cruelty

Whenever you are aware of animal abuse, it's time to polish your wand and get out your candles. The moon phase is irrelevant, and there is no set time during the day that you have to abide by. You will need a piece of black obsidian. This stone will eliminate any wrongdoing and project a protective force to the creature.

### MATERIALS

If you have a picture of the individual causing the cruelty, print it out and place it on your altar before starting the ritual

A knife

A white candle

A black candle

A lighter

A piece of black obsidian

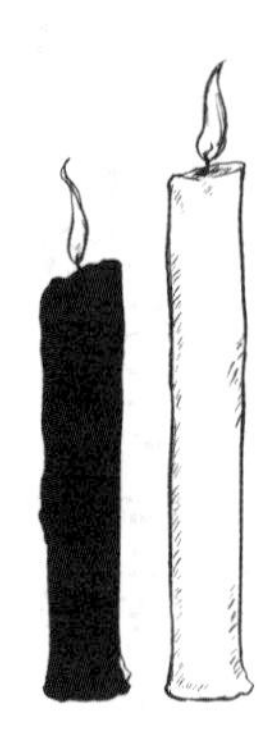

### RITUAL

Take a knife and inscribe the words ANIMAL PROTECTION—STOP ABUSE on the white candle in big capital letters. Next, take the black candle and inscribe the words ABUSER BE STOPPED, again, in large uppercase letters.

Stand the two candles side by side on your altar and light them. Carefully and quickly wave the crystal through the flame of each candle before resting it in front of them.

It's time to meditate and focus on the details of the abuse. It might be hard for you to envision, but this is vital if you want to stop it. If you are an emotional person, try not to cry. You must summon your inner strength because this will add to your power.

Spend a few minutes concentrating on the abuse, and then change your mind-set completely. Now you must visualize the perpetrator being stopped by the authorities. Imagine them being taken far away from the animal. As much as you might despise the person who committed this abuse, you must make sure that you don't send them any ill will. All you want is for the person to be stopped in their tracks; it is the spirit world's job to dish out any punishments, not ours.

Now, move your thoughts back to the animal and see them filled with joy and delight. Watch them running free, playing, being loved by kind people. They are giddy, excited, and confident once more.

Next, you need to summon Ariel, the angel of animals. If you are more inclined to connect with the Gods, the Greek goddess Artemis would be a good choice. Say this incantation seven times while you stare into the flames:

*"[Name of deity] help me with my plight.*
*Bring down your power and make things right.*
*Bless this creature, free it from harm,*
*Send forth the power to my crystal charm."*

When both candles have burned down (don't leave them unattended), take the stone outside and bury it. The power from the angel or goddess will send the magick through the earth to the animal in crisis.

Pets make wonderful friends. They never judge you, will always love you, and will always sense if there is something wrong with you. Their loyalty is pure.

Chapter 12

# Magickal Children

EVERY PERSON CONNECTED TO US IN LIFE IS PART OF our spiritual karma. Before we reincarnate, we are told which lessons we need to learn and are placed with these people, for either our own personal development or for us to help another soul to ascend. Witches, in general, are made of tough stuff, so it is not uncommon for us to have children who are complex and unusual. For the last thirty or forty years, there has been a new wave of child being born on the earth, referred to as Crystal, Star, Rainbow, or Indigo Children. These youngsters stand out among the rest, sometimes for their marvelous talents and also for their behavior, both good or bad. The interesting thing about these particular children is that they have an innate interest in the planet and the environment and tend to look at things in a completely different way from other children. They are extra sensitive as babies and liable to have issues like trouble sleeping or not eating properly. For any young female witches out there, if you decide to venture into motherhood, it is highly likely that you will give birth to at least one of these special children. Raising these kinds of children takes a great deal of dedication and persistence, so you will need to be more proactive as a parent than most other parents.

## THE CRYSTAL CHILD

This child reincarnates with a great deal of empathy. Because their soul is mature, they go on to have a love of nature and all things environmental.

When they are in a countryside environment, they blossom—charging about; hugging trees; and being fascinated by animals and all living things. These youngsters are susceptible to noise and arguments, and parents will have to be on their best behavior, as family disharmony can cause these children mental stress. Many witchy moms give birth to Crystal Children, as witches are often flexible and open-minded, so they're naturally adept at handling a different kind of parenting.

Crystal Children are born with an inner knowledge of all things spiritual and might come out with some strange babblings from a very early age. This might stem from the fact that they are used to the reincarnation process and have visited earth thousands of times in the past. As babies, they might spend ages gazing up at the ceiling, or gurgle and laugh, as if interacting with an invisible person. They can see a spirit, feel a spirit, and, most of all, they can even talk to them.

The Crystal Child has an eclectic taste in music, too, ranging from classical concertos and opera to garage music and pop. They are also gifted in writing or possess original poetry skills. When they are exceptionally small, they may fiddle with things to see how they work or squirrel away little odds and ends when they go about their daily routines. When they are older, they usually go into one of the caring professions, and may become a doctor, a veterinarian, a nurse, a teacher, or a physical therapist.

If a witch has the responsibility of giving birth to and raising a Crystal Child, she has been chosen by the spirit world for this essential and sometimes difficult task. These children are not easy to bring up and can sometimes have behavioral problems—probably because they think differently, or maybe because they don't feel that they are being understood. The usual toddler tantrum you might experience with a regular kid hits a different level with this type of child: they can scream the house down, not letting up for a moment, leaving the parent's nerves in tatters. Yet Crystal Children also have brilliant minds and are adept at thinking outside the box. They have unusual eyes that can stare straight into your soul. The eye color most commonly seen among Crystal Children is bright blue and also hazel, which indicate that they possess psychic abilities.

One of the things that is most interesting is that, as they grow up, many Crystal Children have a strong belief in other worlds and extraterrestrials, and are sometimes extremely interested in astronomy. Most of them are incredibly tech-savvy and obsessed with computers, gadgets, or gaming; they need to exercise their brains rather than their bodies.

Learning in a school or college will not always be a priority, as Crystal Children prefer to individually pursue the things closest to their heart; they have their own personal itinerary to follow. Many parents will have to homeschool them because they might have difficulty fitting in or find it hard to form friendships in their early life. The parents will also have to deal with health issues, such as eczema, allergies, rashes, and skin eruptions. Care must be taken with the products used for these delicate little infants, especially if they get diaper rash. Some are extra sensitive to pollution, and unclean air and even a burning candle can create breathing problems for them.

These challenging and complex little individuals are incredibly loyal and become loving and attentive to their families as they progress into adulthood.

As their name suggests, Crystal Children respond and react strongly to crystals of any kind. Calming amethyst and fluorite can alleviate their frustrations, so it's a good idea to have an extensive collection of these crystals around them. They will gravitate to the ones that please them, being able to easily sense the crystal's vibrational frequencies.

Many extended families have at least one Crystal Child. They teach us to grow and to look at the world differently.

## THE STAR CHILD

The Star Child is similar to the Crystal Child, and may possess many of the same attributes. One recognizable feature of this individual is their physical beauty. They can be breathtakingly stunning, with intense eyes of violet, green, or blue that look right into your heart. Their purpose in life is to raise the human vibration, and because they are "all-knowing" and precocious, they can sometimes appear intimidating to others. From a young age, they are able to recall their past-life memories and may bring up unusual fears that have been carried over from another life. It's a good idea to talk openly to them about any memories they might have as a way of helping them deal with previous issues. Star Children are super psychic from an early age and can often read minds. In later life, they will have a love of all things esoteric and can even go on to be clairvoyants, mediums, or psychics. They may also possess knowledge that they could never know at such a young age, and are thought of as "old souls."

Being highly creative, they adore drawing and painting, and appreciate art in any form. They hate the spotlight, though, so they tend to avoid being in the public eye, preferring to be alone rather than in crowds.

Star Children can take a while to grow up and won't enjoy getting older. If they are pushed too hard, they will become impatient and unhappy, so if you are graced with one of these children it is always best to let them mature at their own pace. These are the empaths of the earth, and they are so sensitive that they can become overly emotional very quickly. As young children, you might want to shield them from any news that is too graphic or explicit, as they will take forever to get over it. In time, this empathetic trait will develop as they get older, and often they will gravitate toward a career in the helping professions, such as a counselor, a therapist, or a psychiatrist. Their aim stems from a desire to help others come to terms with any emotional traumas.

As already mentioned, from a tender age their psychic ability will be apparent, and they might shock the people around them with their uncanny predictions. This ability generally means they have good intuition and the capability to easily read people. They might have an immediate aversion to certain folks they meet without having any prior knowledge of their character, or instantly throw themselves at strangers they take a liking to. This child is a dreamer with one foot on the earth and the other in the spirit world. They experience vivid dreams and will possibly master the art of astral travel by the time they are three or four.

Each Star Child holds a great deal of compassion for human nature and projects a forgiving and loving character. They have a pearl of innate wisdom and a great deal of patience with fellow humans, knowing that there is far more to the world that we think.

They will resonate with their own kind and can spot another Star Child in an instant, often forming friendships with them that last a lifetime. One thing is for certain when you meet this child: you will instinctively know that you are in the presence of someone special.

## THE RAINBOW CHILD

Many Rainbow Children were born around the year 2000 and beyond, so they are rarer than Crystal or Star Children. One belief is that they are new souls free of spiritual baggage carried over from another life, leaving them innocent and open-minded to new things. They are often described as being hyperactive and full of energy: their parents are continually chasing after them, and because of their lack of experience on the earth plane, they have difficulty listening or are badly behaved. Having said that, they are thought to be the healers of the planet, reincarnating to change the vibrational frequencies of the earth and its occupants. This isn't something they physically do; they just naturally project energy to the earth from inside themselves. Another belief is that they have no karma, and their sole purpose in reincarnating is to help others to be more compassionate and to raise awareness of all things relating to the environment. They are here to help humanity grow, but because they are quite recent arrivals, it is not clear as to how they will achieve this.

This child might not speak until they are around three or four and are often misdiagnosed. They have beautiful, large eyes and can be quite withdrawn when they are small, not mixing with others much, leaving them open to being bullied. However, their kind hearts hold no malice, and they'll find it easy to forgive others for any wrongdoing directed their way. They will usually be born into a happy, loving family where members will be tenderhearted and sensitive. This stems from the fact that they hate any kind of drama, preferring gentle parents who are devoted to them.

One of the standout things about this child is their psychic ability and, often, they will take an avid interest in all things esoteric. Once grown up, they have a way of being able to magickally manifest anything they choose, making them excellent spellcasters.

# INDIGO CHILDREN

Witches of any kind are usually the offspring of Indigo people, who are specially chosen by the spirit world to revolutionize the planet. They are born with compassion for the earth, loving plants and animals and all things natural.

From a very early age, the Indigo Child will know psychically that they are special and might even come across as being a little arrogant at times. Like the other children spotlighted in this chapter, they are psychic and can read minds, often exposing lies and untruths. They are able to think ahead and are not likely to be bound by tradition or ancient beliefs. Indigos believe in themselves, despite being out of place with regular folks who might even ridicule their way of life and eccentric beliefs. Some believe them to be "Star Seed" people who have come from a different galaxy. They have magickal powers, especially with any type of healing, whether hands-on or remote.

They are sensitive souls who cry easily if they watch a sad movie or if they witness some kind of injustice; in fact, they are so in tune with their emotions that they always act on gut feelings and instincts. Because they think differently, they often have a hard time in school, not always understanding the traditional ways of teaching. However hard they try, they never quite grasp the concept of rote learning. They are, however, extremely intelligent and will learn best once they leave the classroom environment and make their way into the world. Indigo Children are enthusiastic and curious, and will always be asking their parents "How?" or "Why?" So, as with the other children mentioned in this chapter, they will be a challenge to their parents. As Indigo Children mature, most will take an interest in all things paranormal and may even have a strong belief in aliens and otherworldly entities. They are spiritual without being religious, just as they are somehow born with hidden knowledge about the world and how it works. Many of today's adult witches are much like this, with an inherent understanding of earth and animal harmony, and the universal laws of karma. All these traits are said to be inherited from an Indigo parent.

To all of those witches out there, know you are special and proceed on your path, bringing harmony and healing to your own kind and the planet.

# Afterword

This book was composed during the most harrowing of times. The coronavirus has moved throughout the world, leaving a rush of death and resurrection in its wake. During the height of the Covid-19 pandemic, when much of the world was in lockdown, the planet was briefly able to recuperate, with pollution way down and wildlife rebounding in suburban and urban areas. It's astounding that by grounding humans, much of the earth temporarily reverted to a place that was uncontaminated, beautiful, and pure. We could visibly see the dramatic changes the planet was going through.

Most witches worship the earth and understand that to achieve harmony, everything in life must be in balance. It is doubtful that the virus will completely disappear, but once the world has leveled out, we must all learn from the lessons this crisis has provided us. We need to take care of Mother Earth and cut down on our use of plastic. We must give the oceans a fighting chance. Scientists predict that in the next fifty years, if we continue to live as we do, there will be more plastic in the oceans than there are fish—a horrifying thought! Now is the time to look at how our ancestors behaved and adopt some of the methods they used centuries ago. They revered the earth and used all of nature's elements to enrich their lives.

Today, Wiccans, druids, and pagans naturally lean toward getting back to basics, and many make their own environmentally friendly laundry detergents, soaps, shampoos, and such.

Our hearts go out to all those who didn't survive this pandemic, and their families; the pain suffered when losing a loved one is more than anyone can bear. While writing this book, it has reaffirmed our spiritual beliefs, and we both recognized the importance of taking extra care with our health and well-being, not only physically but mentally. Shawn has spent more time meditating, and Leanna, like many other people the world over, has spent endless hours in the garden, getting back to nature.

We want to leave a message to all the witches of today and the young witchlets who are just coming into the craft: leave your descendants an incredible legacy, teach them all you have learned, and pass on to them the knowledge of self-care. We can all enjoy this technological world, but we do need to incorporate into it what really matters, and that is to look deeper into the spirituality of life.

# Acknowledgments

At Sterling, it takes a witches' brew of wisdom, insight, and seeing into the future to put forth a book that touches the heart and soul of our dedicated readers in the Modern-Day Witch series.

We want to thank our brilliant editor, Barbara Berger, for keeping the cauldron boiling with her editorial magick and vision; and, our agent, Bill Gladstone at Waterside Productions, for lighting the cauldron's fire starting us on our journey.

Of course, we are also grateful to the following people at Sterling for their tireless energy and creative talents: interior designer Christine Heun, project editor Michael Cea, photo editor Linda Liang, production manager Ellen Hudson, art director Jo Obarowski-Burger, creative director Melissa Farris; also designer Amy King for the beautiful cover for Sterling. Thank you for helping to bring our book to life.

# Picture Credits

**Alamy:** World History Archive: front endpaper

**ClipArt ETC:** 16, 23, 80, 103, 105, 107, 118 top, 145, 159, 161, 180, 220 top, 221, 225, 242, 243, 254, 257, 278 right, 280

**Clipart.com:** 199

**Depositphotos.com:** chempina: 233; Katja87: 195

**Fromoldbooks.com:** 170

**Getty Images:** *DigitalVision Vectors:* benoitb: 232 top, 249, back endpaper; clu: 145296, 297; CSA-Printstock: 295; duncan1890: 33, 50, 63, 182, 194, 208, 258, 293; GeorgePeters: 27, 29, 61, 67, 106, 155, 204, 253, 285; Grafissimo: 264, 267, 269; ilbusca: 15 left, 112, 135 bottom, 144, 190, 191, 229 top, 240, 241, 255, 268, 271 bottom, 287; ivan-96: 78; johnwoodcock: 237; KeithBishop: 132; Man_Half-tube: 19, 172, 228 top; MatthewGrove: 278 left; mecaleha: 220 bottom; Nastasic: 115, 167, 171, 219, 234, 281, 291; powerofforever: 76 bottom; pseudodaemon: 21 bottom, 123, 127, 131, 134 top, 136 top; rhoon: 48 left; stefan_Alfonso: 152 left; whitemay: 277; zaricm: 126; ZU-09: 222; *iStock/Getty Images Plus:* Acnakelsy: 230; Alhontess: 31, 111, 186; AlinaMaksimova: 133, 134 bottom; andipantz: 166; angorious: 178; Awispa: 24, 38 right, 59 top, 192; BeatWalk: 168; canicula1: 71; channarongsds: 99, 146; ChrisGorgio: 189; Christine_Kohler: 289; Cofeee: 26; Dencake: 81, 206; denisk0: 108; Aurelija Diliute: 203 top; dimonspace: 187 bottom; Jeanna Draw: 227; Epine_art: 47 top, 148, 149, 152 right, 184 left, 185 top, 246; Fearsonline: 117; geraria: 38 left, 39, 135 top, 136 bottom, 137, 147, 173, 177, 193, 201, 283 middle right; HelgaMariah: 224; Hulinska_Yevheniia: 276; JonnyJim: 72; kameshkova: 215; Lisitsa: 271 top; logarphmic: 185 bottom; Ievgeniia Lytvynovych: 136 middle; Marabird: 212; MarinaVorontsova: 47 bottom, 48 right, 125, 188 left, 190 top; maystra: 129, 165; Mariia Mazaeva: 188 right; mubai: 158 nicoolay: 17; NSA Digital Archive: 6; ONYXprj: 150; paseven: 69; Paul Art: 275; Valeriya Pichgina: 244; Pimpay: 58 bottom, 116, 119, 162, 202, 226, 247, 283 toop right; pleshko74: 174; polygraphus: 140; RinaOshi: 187 top; song_mi: 183 235; suricoma: 58 top; Ukususha: 265; Vasilyevalara: 169; Vladayoung: 59 bottom; Zdenek Sasek: 141; *liquidlibrary:* Jupiterimages: 239 top; *Vetta:* CSA Images: 18 bottom, 210

**Internet Archive:** 153

**Library of Congress:** 5

**The Metropolitan Museum of Art:** 260

**New York Public Library:** 95

**Shutterstock:** alaver: cover, throughout (flower border); Amber_Sun: 49 left; Art N'Lera: 120 top; ARTHA DESIGN: 93; AVA Bitter: 21; Babkina Svetlana: 85, 87; chempina: 13; Eugene Dudar: 15 right, 157; Elena Eskevich: 41; Ezepov Dmitry: throughout (burst); Christos Georghiou: 65; geraria: 156; Hikari: 122; HikaruD88: 83; Jan-ilu: 299; Katarinanh: 36; Kseniakrop: 239 bottom; Kumicheva: 14; Marta Leo: 130; Lopatin Anton: 44, 45; LUMEZA.com: vi; lumyai l sweet: 232 bottom; marssanya: 228 bottom; Martyshova Maria: 84; Aleks Melnik: 120 bottom; MitrushovaClipArt: 251; Morphart Creation: 274; NataLima: 134 middle; nikiteev_konstantin: 205, 286; Hein Nouwens: 164, 197; omtatsat graphic: 109; Parkheta: 86; Vera Petruk: 1, 11, 121 top, 262; pio3: 176; Vera Serg: cover (herbs); Maryna Serohina: 203 bottom; Svetlana Shishkanova: 229 bottom; Liliya shlalpak: 139, 143, 147, 160, 175 left, 184 right; Alena Solonshchikova: 49 right, 52, 283 right bottom, 284; Gorbash Varvara: 55; Very_Very: 70, 98; WinWin artlab: cover, v (moon cycles); Vlada Young: 82, 250; Zanna Art: 175 right; zhekakopylov: 90

**Wellcome Collection:** 76 top

**Courtesy of Wikimedia Commons:** 89, 198, 238, 263, 283 bottom left

# Index

**NOTE:** Page numbers in **bold** indicate summaries of entry characteristics and uses. Page numbers in *italics* indicate specific spells/rituals/recipes. Page numbers in parentheses indicate noncontiguous references.

## D

## G



## H

## N



## O

## P



## Q



## R

## S

# About The Authors

**SHAWN ROBBINS** is the author or coauthor of six books, including *Psychic Spellcraft, The Witch's Way, The Crystal Witch, The Good Witch,* and *Wiccapedia,* which is now used as a reference guide in many online Wicca schools, as well as *The Wiccapedia Spell Deck* and *Wiccapedia Journal*—all in the successful Modern-Day Witch series. She has taught classes about herbs, health, and healing at the New York School of Occult Arts and lectures extensively throughout the country on these subjects. She lives in New York City.

**LEANNA GREENAWAY** is a popular British clairvoyant who has appeared on TV and radio. She is the author or coauthor of numerous books, including *Psychic Spellcraft, The Witch's Way, The Crystal Witch, Wiccapedia,* and *Simply Tarot,* as well as *The Wiccapedia Spell Deck* and *Wiccapedia Journal*. She was a columnist for UK *Fate & Fortune Magazine*. See more at https://leannagreenaway.info/. She lives in Somerset, UK.

NOTES

NOTES